W9-CNX-373

Taste Berries for Teens

INSPIRATIONAL SHORT STORIES AND ENCOURAGEMENT ON LIFE, LOVE, FRIENDSHIP AND TOUGH ISSUES

With contributions from teens for teens

Bettie B. Youngs, Ph.D., Ed.D.

author of *Values from the Heartland, Gifts of the Heart*
and *Taste-Berry™ Tales*

Jennifer Leigh Youngs

SCHOLASTIC INC.
New York Toronto London Auckland Sydney
Mexico City New Delhi Hong Kong

To teens everywhere:
May we honor and protect your *ideals*,
value your *wisdom*, learn from your *experiences*,
and point you in the direction of your *calling*.

We would like to acknowledge the following publishers and individuals for permission to reprint the following material. (Note: The stories that were penned anonymously, that are public domain or were previously unpublished stories written by Bettie B. Youngs or Jennifer Leigh Youngs are not included in this listing. Also not included in this listing but credited within the text are those stories contributed or based upon comments by teens.)

The Paintbrush by Lee Ezell, adapted from *You and Self-Esteem: A Book for Young People.* ©1996 Bettie B. Youngs. Reprinted with permission.

The Dragon in My Drawer!, and *Did I Pass Your Test for Friends?*, by Elmer Adrian. Reprinted with permission.

Equal Pay for Equal Worth, by Bettie B. Youngs. Reprinted with permission by publisher Health Communications, Inc., Deerfield Beach, Florida, from *Gifts of the Heart* by Bettie B. Youngs, Ph.D., Ed.D. ©1996 Bettie B. Youngs, Ph.D., Ed.D.

I Have to Live with Myself and So . . . , *52 Simple Ways to Encourage Others* and *You! Yes, You!* Excerpted from *I CAN Ignite the Community Spirit: 301 Ways to Turn Caring into Action*, by Joy J. Golliver and Ruth Hayes-Arista. ©1997 Joy J. Golliver and Ruth Hayes-Arista. To order call 1-800-254-ICAN. Reprinted with permission.

ISBN 0-439-25613-5

12 11 10 9   3 4 5/0

Printed in the U.S.A.   23

First Scholastic printing, October 2000

Cover illustration and design by Andrea Perrine Brower.

Contents

PART 2: FRIENDSHIP: FINDING, KEEPING AND—SOMETIMES—LOSING IT

PART 4: DECIDING WHAT TO DO IN LIFE: DISCOVERING YOUR INTERESTS, TALENTS AND DIRECTION

PART 5: GIVING, SHARING, MAKING A DIFFERENCE

Acknowledgments

We would like to thank some of the people who were "taste berries" in the development of this book.

To our publisher, Peter Vegso, and the entire staff of Health Communications, Inc. In particular, to the editorial staff—most especially Lisa Drucker, Matthew Diener, Christine Belleris and Erica Orloff—a very special thanks. Not only are they fun to work with, but their encouragement and support on a project of this undertaking is so important. Another special thank-you to Andrea Perrine Brower, who designed the cover of this book, as well as the gorgeous covers of three of Bettie's other books: *Values from the Heartland, Gifts of the Heart* and *Taste-Berry Tales*. And, to Tina Moreno, Cathy Jones and Maria Rios of our staff, for their professionalism and generous support, a most heartfelt thanks. Finally, with much gratitude and respect, we offer a very "taste-berry" thanks to all the teens who worked so diligently on this book with us, proving once again that teens see so clearly from the "eyes of the heart."

We each would like to individually thank some very special people for their support and encouragement while we worked on this book.

Bettie

I'd like to thank some very delicious and important "taste berries" in my life. First and foremost, I must return a heart full of love to my coauthor and daughter, Jennifer Leigh Youngs. Jennifer has always been a special soul mate of mine, and doing this book together taught me—for the second time—the true meaning of the words "labor of love"! To my anchors in all times:

the wisest and most loving woman I have ever known—and the first line of defense on my behalf—my mother Arlene; and one of my best friends—a staunch confidant and wise and very loved old sage—my father Everett. Also, an ever-standing thank-you to my brothers and sisters, and brothers- and sisters-in-law—all of whom are dear to me and so giving of friendship. I never take you for granted. And, to a "perfectly good Texas boy," my husband David. Always, always he is a "taste berry"!

Jennifer

I would like to give glory to God. Walking with him has transformed my life with countless blessings and even a few small miracles. Many times throughout my destiny there was only one set of footprints, always reminding me to look up. And, I'd like to thank my parents for loving me as they do. Growing up isn't easy, and I'm sure there were times when they wondered what spaceship dropped me off! Thank you for seeing me through all the tough times and for all the support and unconditional love—and for the conditional love as well. Thank you for having my best interest at heart—always, I know that I am loved! I am lucky to have you both, a fact that becomes clearer to me with each passing year.

To you, Dad (Dic Youngs), thanks for being my friend and protector. Even though as a teen I didn't appreciate your telling my dates that they'd "better have my daughter home on time" (and then reminding them that you could use the baseball bat that sat in the corner), I so appreciate that part of your heart that loves me enough to oversee that I am safe in the world. You will always be my hero and I will always "go to bat" for you. You have shown me what to look for in a "good guy": integrity, honesty, loyalty, friendship, humor—and a great voice! And, Dad, thanks for that tone of voice and that look in your eyes when you say, "That's my girl!" It's been worth more than you know.

To my mother (Bettie Youngs), who has taught me the value of loving myself, and helped me find the courage to forgive the parts of me that I don't accept and helped me come to believe that, in the end, it is the brightness of the light within that counts. There was a time when I didn't want to be like you, and a time when I feared that I wouldn't be. You have helped me "see" the person I am, and you have modeled the woman I hope to become. Thanks for loving me as you do: it shows in everything you do—like giving me the opportunity to coauthor this book. Working together has been so much fun, so fulfilling, so cherished.

Thanks to my dear friend Tawny Pearl Flippen—best friends always. And, to Turtle, Frog, White Light. And, to Ron Young, whose heart ventures past the surface and into the spirit, "seeing" the good in everyone—as you say, "Life is good." And, to the friends I didn't mention—you know who you are and how much I value your friendship. You are true "taste berries" and you make my life sweeter.

Preface

I had just completed *Taste-Berry Tales*, a book of short stories for adult readers highlighting some of the many wonderful ways people make a difference in the lives of others. After a number of people had read the book, many suggested that it would be a wonderful idea to do a book specifically for young people, highlighting some of the many things teens do to become caring, responsible people, and ways they make a difference in the lives of others—and in the world. Having been a classroom educator, and experiencing firsthand the parenting of an adolescent myself—and having had so many of her friends constantly in my home—I knew so well that teenagers greatly contribute to the betterment of others, and their perspective on life and living is a valued one. Though I was very interested in doing a book for teens, I had other pressing matters and a heavy travel schedule. In short, it hadn't reached my "Must Do" list.

But the idea refused to go away and, curiously, it insisted on having voice—a persistent one. That voice increased in volume during Christmas when I received a holiday letter from my friend, Colleen Morey, a program administrator in Connecticut. In her letter, Colleen described an experience she'd had with a group of young people, many of whom were jaded, and had pretty much given up on life, so much so that some of them called themselves "losers." To enlist their enthusiasm (and so that they would learn to use the computer), Colleen linked her students up with another group of young people—living in Bogotá, Colombia!

In "talking" and sharing with each other, Colleen's students learned that the kids in Bogotá were living in an orphanage and had never once so much as received a present or gift from anyone in their entire lives. The American teenagers were surprised—and empathetic. It was unthinkable to them to be without the basics—CDs, several pairs of shoes, clothes they liked and had chosen for themselves, a room of their own and foods they liked (staples like pizza, hamburgers and french fries). Colleen's students decided to do something to change the plight of their newfound friends.

So they began collecting boxes upon boxes of clothing, books, CDs (very big on their list!), medical supplies and other things they felt these young people should have. Several months and some fifty-plus boxes later, Colleen's students were ready to send these items to their friends in Bogotá. This presented a new challenge: How would they afford to send the many boxes to Bogotá?

At the same moment this challenge presented itself, out of the blue, Leeanne Hansen (Colleen's former college friend) called Colleen to say she'd been thinking about her and wanted to renew their friendship. Having lost track of where Colleen was living, Leeanne had called Colleen's parents for her phone number. The two friends talked by phone and discussed the possibility of getting together. "How about tomorrow?" Leeanne suggested. "It just so happens I am on my way to the East Coast, and as luck would have it, I'll be in the very city where you now live."

The two former friends and schoolmates, who had not seen or spoken with each other for nearly ten years, were reunited and had the chance to catch up on all that was going on in their lives. You can only imagine their intrigue when Colleen told Leeanne of her current work, including the challenge to help her students find a way to transport the items they had collected for the children in Bogotá, Colombia—especially since Leeanne was coordinator for Airline Ambassadors (founded by her friend Nancy Rivard), a volunteer group that provides humanitarian assistance to children around the world. Wouldn't you know it, with the return of Leeanne into Colleen's life came the resolution of the problem of how to deliver the boxes to Bogotá. During Christmas break, Colleen and Leeanne delivered the boxes, courtesy of Airline Ambassadors!

When I read Colleen's Christmas letter, I was so moved by it that I called her to learn more about it and to tell her that she must share her story. "What incredible timing," Colleen declared. "This past week my students have created a new goal: Ever more fired up by their efforts, they want to share their story with others, hoping that other young people around the world will be inspired to do similar things. In fact, they'd like to solicit students from other schools—maybe even from around the world—but we don't know how to get the word out."

"Your timing is perfect," I said. "I can help you. What a coincidence that I'm writing a book for young people, one that will be published in a number of foreign countries. . . ." And so this book made it to my "To Do" list. No sooner had I added it to my list than my daughter called and said, "Mom, I'm working with teens around the country and I'd like to share the things I've learned with teens—so let's do a book. . . ."

Coincidences? Maybe. But perhaps even more is going on than meets the eye—like, synchronicity. Synchronicity is a word used to describe a meaningful coincidence of two or more events where something other than the probability of chance is involved. The overall effect leaves us with the feeling that the sequence of events has to be more than coincidence. And that's exactly what happened here. As if orchestrated by divine intervention, each person who needed to carry out the next necessary step appeared when needed. If we watch closely, and most especially if we are looking for it, we will find that synchronicities happen in our lives quite frequently, like in the creation of *Taste Berries for Teens*.

Introduction

Why *Taste Berries for Teens*? A taste berry is a glorious little fruit that convinces the taste buds that all food—even food that is distasteful—is delicious. The bright little berry has been used by aboriginal tribes around the world for countless years to make the sometimes necessary eating of bitter roots—and grubs—tolerable. On some days, we could all use a taste berry!

The good news is that people can be "taste berries" to each other. Has someone said a kind word or done some deed that made a victory more satisfying, a joy sweeter, a broken heart less painful? If so, that person was acting as a taste berry. When we help others—such as by being a great friend—we sweeten life's joys and ease the bitterness of its disappointments and losses.

Teens know plenty about being taste berries. From sending a thank-you note to earning merit badges; from helping a friend sort out feelings during a time of personal turmoil to supporting a friend through her parents' divorce; from helping each other with homework to deciding what each wants to do after high school and beyond; from rescuing a lizard to serving the homeless in soup kitchens and building Habitat Homes throughout the world—teens are taste berries to others. And, as a result, they are changing the world.

This book is organized into seven parts, with stories and comments from teens within each part. Each chapter focuses on a theme, which is presented in the chapter's opening by means of a lead-in story or parable. This is followed by a section called "A Word from the Authors," which previews the chapter coming up—giving a glimpse of the highlights of some of its other stories, as well as clarifying the chapter's theme for teens. After this section, there are the comments from teens, edited first by teens for content, then by the authors. We asked teens nationwide to send us their stories, as well as to read and rate each other's stories. Young people from the ages of twelve to twenty from across the United States read and critiqued individual stories, and commented or shared a story or example of their own. In some cases, we worked within schools and got to meet many teens firsthand.

The stories and comments we received represent the personal opinions of the teens who shared them. (Keep in mind that this was a diverse group—both male and female—of varying ages and backgrounds.) As such, they do not necessarily reflect our own opinions, nor are we suggesting that the reader should necessarily agree with them. Nor do the stories in this book represent the full range and scope of the many issues that today's teens face. We'd also like to stress that many of the situations described would be tough for any of us to handle—no one expects teens to go it alone. In this book you'll meet other teens who are dealing with tough challenges and you'll learn how they are working through them. Although some of these teens figured out what to do on their own, others needed to turn to friends, family and professionals to give them a hand.

Teens can find themselves sorting out things that seem overwhelming—whether it's because they are feeling like they don't "measure up," are facing serious and life-changing issues, are handling day-to-day stresses and strains, or are dealing with a combination of any of these. If you are facing struggles that seem overwhelming, rather than suffer alone or resort to doing things that are self-destructive, we urge you to confide in an adult you trust. This is especially true in the cases of physical or sexual abuse, suicidal feelings, eating disorders, depression, pregnancy and/or using drugs or alcohol. Remember that parents, teachers and other professionals—such as school nurses or counselors—were once teens (and many are now the parents of teens) and know what it feels like to be unsure of oneself, to have fears and anxieties about coping with life in general. Because adults *remem-*

ber, we feel honored to help young people find healthy, supportive ways to deal with their lives. Trust that adults have the best interest of teens at heart and want to help you make the best possible choices when dealing with whatever is going on in your life. If in the past you had an unpleasant or painful experience because an adult seemed aloof to your needs—or even broke your trust—it can be helpful to remember that, fortunately, adults unsympathetic to helping teens are the exception, not the rule.

During those times when everything in your life seems bleak, it's important to give yourself permission to be extra good to yourself—that means resting and eating properly, exercising to stay fit and release tension, and being patient with yourself. You'll find that if you take care of yourself, and reach out to those you know will offer friendship, understanding and guidance, you will be able to use a difficult experience to help you learn to develop healthy responses for coping with life's challenges. If you're uncertain where to go for counseling, turn to an adult (whether a parent, teacher, school guidance counselor or clergyman) whom you feel you can trust to direct you to the proper place. Also, many schools provide peer crisis counseling, which offers teens valuable support. Learning how to cope effectively can help you become a happy person and develop compassion for others. This is how to become a greater taste berry to yourself and to others.

We look forward to your—our readers'—letters and comments. We welcome hearing which of these stories touched you and which ones you liked best. We'd also love to hear about the taste berries in your lives—or how you've learned to be better taste berries in the lives of others. We're working on *Taste Berries for Teens II*, so if you have stories you'd like to submit for consideration, please send them to us at:

Taste Berries for Teens II
c/o Tina Moreno
3060 Racetrack View Drive
Del Mar, CA 92014

"Taste Berries" *to you!*

Part 1

Self-Worth

Our life is like a piece of paper
on which every passerby leaves a mark.

—Ancient Chinese Proverb

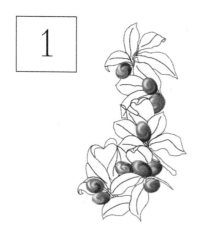

1

Who I (Really) Am

Every artist dips his brush into his own soul, and paints his own nature into his picture—as he does in living his life.

—Henry Ward Beecher

THE PAINTBRUSH

I keep my paintbrush with me, wherever I may go,
In case I need to cover up, so the real me doesn't show.
I'm so afraid to show you me; afraid of what you'll do,
I'm afraid you'll laugh or say mean things; afraid I might lose you.
I'd like to remove all the layers, to show you the real, true me,
But I want you to try to understand; I need you to like what you see.
So if you'll be patient and close your eyes, I'll remove the coats real slow,
Please understand how much it hurts, to let the real me show.
Now that my coats are all stripped off, I feel naked, bare and cold,

And if you still find me pleasing, you are my friend, pure as
    gold.
I need to save my paintbrush though, and hold it in my hand,
I need to keep it handy in case someone doesn't understand.
So please protect me, my dear friend, and thanks for loving me
    true,
And please let me keep my paintbrush with me, until I love me,
    too.

A Word from the Authors

Each of us longs to "be ourselves." And yet, we seek the
approval of others: "Do you think I'm okay?" "Do you accept me
as I am?" "Do you like the way I look?" "Do you approve of how
I act?" "Do you like me?" "Will you be my friend?" We want the
answers to each of these questions to be a wholehearted "Yes!"
When others like us and accept us, we feel worthy—like we're a
terrific person. But even though we may want to feel liked and
accepted by others, we may not always get a positive response—
some people may not think as much of us as we would like.
Sometimes this doesn't bother us, but most of the time, especially if their approval is important to us, it's only natural to feel
rejected, hurt or left out.

All of us are vulnerable to the scrutiny of others. Why are we
so sensitive to their review of us? We want them to accept and
approve of who we are at our inner level, not just for what they
see of us at the surface. What we really want is for others to like
and accept us for *who* we are—*as* we are. But what if they don't
like what they see? The fear of being rejected is at the heart of
the struggle between hiding and revealing ourselves—and can
cause teens to feel as though even the people closest to them
don't really understand them very well.

Almost all of the teens we heard from said that in order to win
favor and friendship from others, they had to "play into" or

portray an image they believe someone else holds of them, rather than "be themselves." It's a coat of paint teens aren't all that happy about wearing: The price-tag for being "someone else" comes at a loss of true identity. Sometimes the loss includes self-respect and self-esteem—your own. The good news is, while you are willing to do *some* things to gain acceptance, there's a limit—and then you begin to feel uncomfortable about it. Feeling uneasy about covering up who you are in order to be liked by someone else is a healthy feeling. You are *you*—and that is who you are supposed to be. You shouldn't have to become someone you're not.

As we read the stories for this unit, my daughter and I talked at length about how easy it is for the image we hold of ourselves to be influenced or colored by others. "When you're a teenager, you get pulled in a lot of different directions, especially when you're trying to meet the expectations of different people—all of whom are important to you," Jennifer commented. "There's a fine line between going along, doing the things others want you to do, and being true to yourself—listening to your own voice and preferences, acting on what you believe, and doing what's important and best for *you*."

"Give me an example," I prompted.

"Well, let's take the image I had of myself as an athlete in high school, more specifically, as a pitcher on my school softball team," she responded. "Just before I'd wind up to throw a pitch, I'd look up in the bleachers and see your smiling face, confident I'd strike out the batter. You'd reinforce it by shouting, 'You can do it, Jen!' Meanwhile I was thinking, 'I just hope this pitch goes somewhere in the direction of the plate and not a half-mile over the batter's head and out of the ballpark entirely!' I wasn't nearly as certain as you were of my pitching skills. Then I'd look over at Dad who had reminded me—on more than one occasion—'Jen, you're better at soccer. That's your best chance for a scholarship. That's where you should be concentrating your time.' All the while, I was wishing I could concentrate on my first love—tennis.

"Once a friend of mine asked me if my favorite sport was softball, soccer or tennis. 'Softball,' I answered. But I thought about it for a minute and knew softball *wasn't* my favorite sport. My answer was based on the gratification I felt having you at my games, and your enthusiasm about my playing softball. On the way home from the games, whether our team won or lost, you thought I played well. In your eyes, I could do no wrong. It was a very good feeling.

"Correcting myself, I said to my friend, 'Actually, I prefer soccer.' But once again, I realized that there were conditions around my playing soccer that made me continue to play it. A couple of times a week, and sometimes on the weekends, Dad spent time with me, teaching me soccer tricks. And, he came to practically every soccer game and once, after one of the games, he told me I was 'the most powerful athlete on the team.' You see, having you and Dad attend my games was the biggest appeal of my playing softball and soccer. It was your presence and approval, not the sport itself, that kept me playing these sports. Now tennis—that was my favorite sport when it came to playing for the fun of it."

"But you received a letter in softball and soccer—because you were so good at them," I reminded her.

"Well, you guys were at practically all the games!" Jennifer said, laughing. "It was just great to look in the bleachers and see one or both of my parents there. Whenever I saw you, that was my favorite game, and my favorite sport."

"So why didn't you play on the tennis team, then?" I asked, bewildered that as a parent, living with her as closely I did, I hadn't picked up on how *she* really felt about each of these sports at the time.

"Simple," she said. "I did play tennis for a while, but the tennis games were mostly held out of town. Since our team took the bus, you and Dad weren't able to come."

I must have looked forlorn, because Jennifer added, "Don't feel bad, Mom. I'll bet there are very few kids who sit at the piano when they're first learning to play, saying, 'I'm practicing for the next half-hour without complaining because I see myself as a great pianist, the next Beethoven.' More likely they're saying, 'I'm practicing because in thirty minutes, I'll get a hug, a bowl of ice cream, time with my friends, an hour of television—and avoid being in trouble with my mom (or dad) for not practicing!'

"And by the way, you two (parents) weren't the only conflicting voices that I had to deal with. There were expectations of friends and coaches. For example, in the dugout was my best friend—also a pitcher—who each game prodded, 'Jennifer, work it so that in the fourth inning I can come in and relieve you!' Which meant, of course, that I was to deliberately pitch a succession of 'balls' and not strikes, so the coach would send me to the dugout and her to the mound. Then there was the coach who said, 'Just do your best'—right before he promised that if we had a good game, he'd take the team out for pizza. Now I had to deal with the question, 'What should I do—am I a good best friend, or a determined pitcher?' So you see, being pulled in so many directions by so many people—all of whom you genuinely want to please—makes having a paintbrush seem like a necessity!"

Perhaps that's what made "The Paintbrush" such a popular piece with teens! We received so many poignant and heartfelt letters from teens everywhere who said "The Paintbrush" described their feelings to a "T," that we felt obliged to make it the first selection in this book! Teens everywhere said, "being a teenager is tough stuff"—one of the biggest reasons being that parents, teachers and even your friends see you differently than you see yourself. In the following stories in this chapter, you'll learn that the struggle to gain acceptance, to be liked and considered worthy without having to be someone else—without having to "cover up"—is a challenge for both girls and boys, whether you are thirteen or eighteen—or ninety! "The Dragon in

My Drawer!" was written just this past year by your friend, nine-ty-year-old Elmer Adrian, who admitted, "The image others see is not the authentic me."

Hmmm, maybe it's a view everyone shares throughout their lives!

Like paint, the views teens shared about being your "authentic self" came in various shades, too. Some of you wanted a paintbrush to cover up, such as sixteen-year-old Shaun Martin, who confessed he needed one "until the *real me . . .* will stay around long enough for me to get used to." Being a teen means constantly growing and changing in many ways. Sometimes many layers of paint were needed for more than camouflage—they were needed as protection. This was true for fourteen-year-old Mia Templett, who tells us *why* each day she paints a smile on her face, and for thirteen-year-old Alana Ballen, recently diagnosed with bipolar disorder. As we suggested in the introduction to this book, when facing problems of so serious a nature, we urge any teen to turn to a trusted adult for help and guidance. Hopefully, as a result of receiving such support, both Mia and Alana can look forward to lighter colors—and brighter days. And many teens, like sixteen-year-old Rebecca Holbrook, thought that perhaps adults, too, cover up their real selves, as she feels her mother does because her mom's "life didn't really turn out the way she wanted."

Other teens were tired of needing a paintbrush and wanted to lay theirs down, to stop being someone else's shade of friend, as did fifteen-year-old Marie Benton. So enthralled that she'd been chosen to do a school project with the all-popular Heather Winslow, Marie found herself shamelessly parading up and down the library, mimicking Heather—even though she knew her actions were suspect! It's nice to see that Marie, like so many teens, is developing the courage to act in ways that feel right to *her.*

While some of you learn lessons firsthand, some learn them

by watching others, like fifteen-year-old Chelsey Collinsdale, whose sister told conflicting stories about wanting a pager to wear to school. As Chelsey tells us, "You have to decide how willing you are to sacrifice your true self in order to have others like you." Still, other teenagers, like sixteen-year-old Chad Dalton, said, "My true color comes out when I'm with *real* friends," and tells us what "color" it takes to be considered his friend. And Eric Chadwick, seventeen, discovered that when it came to the beautiful girl he wanted to date, it was he, and not the girl, who had done the painting! Perhaps Christina's rudeness was her paintbrush—maybe this beautiful girl didn't *feel* all that beautiful. This is a good reason *not* to judge a book by its cover, whether the cover looks appealing or unappealing.

All in all, you said you want to be true to your own color—the self you know better than anyone else does. You want to do as legend Elton John did; he found a newer, wiser, healthier self after getting a fresh look at who he was beneath the layers of paint he had added over the years to meet the expectations of others. You proclaimed what singer-songwriter Stevie Nicks declared: "This is who I really am—and who I want to be."

There is one thing all teens do agree on though: You may, on occasion, wear a coat of paint, but beneath its surface is a self you deeply love and honor. And would like the rest of us to love and honor, too.

Until then, you ask for understanding in keeping your paintbrush handy until you've learned the art of balancing the need for acceptance without sacrificing your own sense of self. In the meantime, please don't give up on the rest of us, who, like your friend ninety-year-old Elmer Adrian, are trying to find the courage to put our paintbrush down, too!

Will the Real Me Please Stand Up!

Lately I've started to wonder what it means when people say, "Just be yourself!" It's a dumb thing to say to me right now because most of the time *I'm* not sure *who* I am! How can I be? I'm constantly changing. I mean, I look and sound totally different than I did just three months ago. Then I had a decent complexion; now it's oily and zit-ridden. Three months ago, my voice sounded like a normal human being's; now it fluctuates between squeaky one day and deep the next—like I'm echoing into a big drum or something. And some of my body parts look like they don't belong with the other parts. I started working out last year, so I was really buffed. But I've grown five inches in the last six months, so I'm gangly and look completely out of proportion. I'm happy about getting taller, except that now my muscles don't look as big and my head looks as if it's sitting on a tall skinny post.

I used to have no problem getting girls to come up and talk with me. Now I've lost confidence that they find me attractive. I worry that if by chance a girl should get interested, it'll only be a matter of time before she'll be turned off by my skin breaking out so much, or laugh when my voice does its squeak-and-croak act.

It's not just my body that has changed—*everything* has. I've always thought of myself as a regular guy; but now, from one day to the next, my emotions are all over the place. One day I feel up, the next down. Some days I think, "Hey, I'm really quite smart," and others, "I'm as dumb as a rock!" One week I'm sure what I want to do with my life, the next, I'm totally unsure. I'm a wreck! Really, I just want the real me to please stand up and stay around long enough for me to get used to him.

Oh yeah, I need a paintbrush for sure!

Shaun Martin, 16

Are You Going to Get a Pager?

I don't "suck up" to others as much as I used to, mostly because of watching how obvious it is to others when someone does suck up. In fact, I've learned quite a bit about paintbrushes lately—from my sister, of all people. My older sister is acting like a yo-yo, being one person around her family, and then like someone completely different when she's with her friends. I realized from watching her that I've done that sometimes, too. When she's with her friends, my sister acts and says things practically the opposite of the way she really is.

I think my sister works way too hard to fit in with her friends. She agrees with them even when they say things that are totally stupid or definitely wrong, or completely opposite of what she believes. Like last week, for example, my sister and I were talking about how many of our friends have pagers. I told her I wanted one. My sister said she thought it was dumb that kids in junior high and high school had them, especially wearing the pager to school, since most of your friends are at school anyway. As she said, "Why would they page you when they could see you in the halls and in class?" I agreed with her. I mean, it's not like your parents are going to page you when you're in class!

But the next day after school, when two of her friends came over to our house, my sister told her friends she thought wearing a pager to school was totally cool and she couldn't wait to get one. When I reminded her that just the evening before she thought a pager was a dumb idea, she stared at me—and if looks could kill, I'd be dead! "You're such a pest!" she snapped, "Why don't you get lost!"

Usually my sister and I get along really well and are good friends. She wouldn't have said that to me if she wasn't trying to impress her friends.

When her friends left, I asked her if she really had changed her mind about wanting a pager to wear to school. "No," she said. "But both of my friends have pagers and wear them to school, so I didn't want to tell them that I thought it was a dumb idea."

"Well, if you do get a pager," I told her, "that is, if Mom and Dad even allow you to get one, you know they'd make you pay for it out of your allowance."

"I know," she said. "And besides, I have an answering machine. That works just as well."

So you see, my sister just told her friends what she thought they wanted to hear. I couldn't figure out why my sister wimped out! Personally, I don't want to work that hard to have friends. I mean, what would be so terrible about my sister believing one thing about kids having pagers and her friends believing something different? Besides, when your friends know where you stand in terms of how you feel or what you think is cool or uncool, they respect you. At least show respect for yourself by sticking up for what you believe in. And even if they don't agree with you, good friends will think you're cool for being true to yourself. That's just the way it is. I think that if your friends don't like that you think a little different than they do, then maybe you shouldn't want them as friends. And, you should consider the loss of friendship their loss, not yours.

I'm not saying that it doesn't bother me when someone doesn't like me or doesn't want to be my friend because I won't go along with everything they say or do. It's just that sometimes you have to "count the cost" as my mother says, and take a stance about how willing you are to sacrifice your opinion of things just to have others like you. Besides, it's a lot of work to keep up a front that isn't really who you are. To me, when you do that it's like painting a coat over the shade you really are.

Chelsey Collinsdale, 15

The Most Beautiful Girl . . .

We don't always see others the way they are, but rather, as we want them to be. I thought Christina Thomas was the most beautiful girl I had ever seen. It took me a long time to get up the courage to ask her out. Finally, I did. When she accepted, I thought I was the luckiest guy in the world. The feeling was short-lived.

The first couple of times I went out with Christina, I was so nervous (and happy to be with her) that I pretty much just agreed with whatever she said. But as I began to relax around her, I saw a person who was very different from what I had imagined.

I was surprised to discover Christina wasn't very respectful of other people. She was always saying mean things about them, always putting them down. And she was rude to people for no reason.

I only went out with Christina for five weeks.

Now I see the real Christina. I know what Christina Thomas is really like, and I don't think she is nearly as pretty as I thought at first.

I think it's possible to wear two coats of paint, one on the outside and one on the inside. The coat of paint Christina has on the outside is awesome, the one on the inside isn't as impressive. Seeing her beauty, I thought she must "be" beautiful, but I've learned that people aren't always what they appear to be. But I doubt that Christina Thomas was ever any different with me than she was with others.

I think that maybe it wasn't Christina who had the paintbrush. I was the one who had painted Christina in a "color" she was not.

Eric Chadwick, 17

The Dragon in My Drawer!

Sometimes when I'm a bit uptight
from doing everything just right,
I have a room, my own retreat
where I can kick my shoes off of my feet.

My desk is cluttered and piled high,
even the curtains are awry.
When I look at this untidy mess,
"Yes!" I shout. I like it, I do confess.

There are things tossed on the floor,
a dragon's in my dresser drawer.
He guards the clothes not folded right
and warns, "Hands off or I shall bite!"

Then, before I leave my room, I comb my hair
and straighten out the things I wear.
But I'll tell you what—that prim and proper image others see
is not the authentic me!

Elmer Adrian, 90

Heather's Clone

At times, I cover up the "real me" by acting in ways I think the other person wants or expects me to, rather than acting on who I really am. I did it just yesterday.

I woke up yesterday feeling sort of "blah"—feeling kind of sick, but not sick enough to stay home. I would have preferred to stay in bed, but I went to school anyway since I didn't want to fall behind in my homework and have to do extra over the weekend. I got up late, showered, got dressed in a hurry, ran my fingers through my hair and rushed out the door. Needless to say, I didn't look my best.

Luckily, my first-period teacher didn't have anything ambitious in mind for us. Our class mostly worked on individual assignments at our own desks. I was not so lucky in my second-period class. The teacher, Mrs. Whetherill, took our class to the library and assigned us to work in pairs on a research project. I was paired with Heather Winslow!

Heather is one of *the* most popular girls at school. Some people might call her selective; others might call her uppity. And preppy. Since I'm just one of the average kids at school, Heather smiles when she sees me, but that's about it. It's not like I'm someone she'd consider hanging around with.

Like everyone else, I'd do almost anything to be her friend (or even to be seen with her). And that's pretty much what I did yesterday!

Heather is a perky sort of person, so even though I wasn't feeling all that well, I put on my I've-got-a-great-personality-and-attitude act. I tried to perk up and be Heather's clone—so she wouldn't mind getting stuck with me for the project. But my transformation didn't end there! The teacher allowed us to walk around the library to get the different reference books we needed for our assigned projects. The two books Heather and I needed were easy to find. But even though we had all the reference books we needed for the project, that didn't stop Heather from pretending we needed others. Heather walked back and forth across the entire length of the library several times—to be seen, of course. I was so happy to be seen with Heather Winslow that I followed her on these aimless jaunts, no doubt looking conspicuous since Heather is more experienced in this sort of thing than I am. I never was quite sure when to appear busy looking for books, or, once I'd attracted attention to myself, when to smile at everyone since it was obvious I had distracted them into noticing me. Heather, of course, had it figured out: She did both.

But I didn't just stop at being Heather's shadow, either! I also tried to sound like her!

Heather giggles all the time. It's a sort of a high-pitched, peculiar sound, one she uses more for getting attention than anything else. So as she walked around searching for bogus reference books, Heather giggled loudly enough to get the attention of other students as she walked by them. And so did I! I mimicked Heather's giggle even though I'm not someone who normally giggles at every little thing. I'm sure that I sounded totally ridiculous, since they'd never heard these strange, quirky little sounds coming from my mouth before. I hadn't either!

At the time, it was fun. Since I was with Heather, *everyone* looked at us. The problem was, because I didn't feel all that great in the morning, I hadn't bothered to put on anything nicer than jeans, an old sweatshirt and my ratty pair of tennis shoes. My hair looked absolutely awful; it was having a bad day, too. Nevertheless, here I was giggling and parading around, drawing attention to myself. I'm sure I looked as ridiculous as I sounded.

Being seen with Heather and getting as much attention as she was (or at least more than I was used to) felt good—yesterday, that is. Today I'd describe my feelings about my behavior in the library more as embarrassed than anything else. I know my classmates knew I was showing off, and even worse, I know I was. It's just that sometimes—even when you know you're acting like a dweeb—it's hard not to get caught up in someone else's behavior. Especially when you're with someone like Heather, who has a way of making you feel like you're obligated to go along with whatever she's doing or saying. It's like the chameleon going along with the colors in its surroundings.

Sometimes I feel like a chameleon, changing my colors when I'm around different kinds of people. When I'm not feeling super secure with myself, I tend to act more or less intelligent, athletic or pretty than I really am. To try to blend in with whoever I'm with, I cover up the "real me" by acting in ways I think the other person wants me to. That's what happened when I got paired up with Heather.

Sometimes you have to do what your friends expect of you because if you don't, you won't have any friends. I know I followed Heather around and tried to be her clone in order to be liked by her. But, you know what, it didn't work. The next day Heather acted like she didn't know me! All that work for nothing!

At least I'm aware of what I did—not that it's much of a consolation. I do want to be more true to myself and not have to paint myself over to be someone else's "color." What I'd really like is for Heather to think I'm so cool she'll follow me around and want to be my clone! Now that's a color I'd like to see.

Marie Benton, 15

The Mask She Wears

Reading "The Paintbrush" made me feel sad for my mother. She works very hard at two jobs and is usually so tired. She has zero social life. Still, she tries to sound upbeat and positive—way more than she really feels. I think her life didn't really turn out the way she wanted, and that she hides a lot of disappointments. I know she doesn't like either one of her jobs. And she doesn't like the house we live in. It needs painting and new carpet and a lot of repairs, things we can't afford to do right now. Mom says we should get a newer, smaller place, but a newer, smaller house can't really fix things because the real problem is that Mom doesn't want to live in this town any longer. She and my father divorced last year, and my mother would like to move back near her parents. But I really like the school I go to and I like my friends. When my mother was my age, her father's company transferred him to a different city. She had to leave her friends behind and complete high school in a whole new area. Mom said it was a terrible experience for her. She told me that she doesn't want me to have to go through the same thing. So we're going to stay here until I finish high school. I like that idea, but I know it's tough on my mother, one more compromise she's making. Even though Mom acts like it's okay with her, I know it isn't. It must not be much fun to be her.

I appreciate all the things my mother does for me. I know she works hard at trying to make the best of our situation. I'm trying to do my part, too. I'm trying to complain less about the things I want but know we can't really afford, such as a phone of my own. And I'm trying to be a little more understanding and patient with my mom when she's stressed out.

I guess that sometimes adults have to be someone other than who they'd prefer to be. Sometimes adults paint on a mask, too.

Rebecca Holbrook, 16

Quiet and Shy—Not!

I know there are times when my parents and teachers—even some of my friends—see me differently than I *really* am. They think I'm quiet and shy, really smart but not very cool. What they don't know is that's who I am when I am with them, but it's not who I *really* am. The *real* me comes out when I'm around guys who are more like me—like Tom Henderson and Graham Barry. Tom and Graham bring out the best in me, the real me.

I met Tom and Graham at a *Young Scientist* contest last year. Tom is from Orem, Utah, and Graham is from Ontario, California. The three of us were among the five finalists in a national competition for *Promising New Scientists*. As soon as the three of us met, we really hit it off. As we talked about the conference, we discovered that all three of us were interested in laser space debris mitigation, which is the study of the prevention of space garbage damaging satellites and the new space station. It was great to meet other people my age who actually knew what I was talking about. When I talk about "space garbage," most of the kids at my school just say, "Oh, you mean like asteroid-type things? I played a video game about that once."

Luckily, we met each other on the first day of the conference, so we were able to spend a lot of time together for the entire three days. We ate all our meals together, went to each others' event showings, and went out and saw a little of the city together. Then when we'd get back, even though it was late, we'd talk until 2:00 or 3:00 A.M. It was great! We talked about everything from the best schools to go to, what degrees to get, the kind of jobs we want, and even the names of the best people in each field. We want to study with the pioneers. Both Tom and I want to study with Dr. Claude Phipps from Santa Fe, New Mexico. He's the inventor of ORION, a space debris mitigation company that developed a laser that knocks down space garbage before it does any damage to expensive space vehicles. Some of the space garbage travels at over one thousand miles per second! Although you can't track something as small as a grain of sand, it can still do some real damage. Graham wants to study under Jim Cronin, the physics Nobel Laureate from the University of Chicago.

Even though the three of us don't get a chance to see each other very often, we're still the best of friends. We're always sending articles and newspaper clippings to each other, and sometimes we'll send a copy of a class paper we think the other would find interesting. And we call each other a couple of times a month. That may not sound like a lot of time together, but even so, Tom and Graham are better friends of mine than any of the kids I see every day at school. And they know me better than any of the kids at school know me. The three of us just really understand each other and where we're coming from.

I have more fun with them than anyone else. When I get a phone call or email from either Tom or Graham, it's the best feeling—a real high. I always feel happy and in a good mood, even when I'm working through a problem, when I talk with Tom and Graham. It's like this other person in me wakes up. With them, I'm my "real shade."

Chad Dalton, 16

Love, *Me*

I once wrote my girlfriend a letter and signed it "Just me." It surprised me when she told me she didn't like the way I signed it. "I'd rather go out with someone who thought more of himself than 'just me,'" she commented. "I deserve more than a 'just me' boyfriend."

What she said made me realize that when I wrote "just me," I was really saying "I'm no one special." But that's not how she feels about me, and it's not how I feel about myself, either. When I thought about it, I realized that I underestimated the importance of talking (and writing) about myself in a positive way.

So I'm giving myself a whole new "paint job." I've decided to stop (unconsciously) putting myself down. Before, I'd say things like, "School isn't for me, I'm a horrible student." Even saying or thinking those words made me feel like I was a horrible student and so I'd dislike school even more—which was crazy because it wasn't even true. I'm not a bad student. And I don't hate school. I'm a bright guy, and I like most of my classes.

Now I say things in a better way, a way that doesn't make me get down on myself. Now when I talk about school, I say something like, "I like school even though I'm having a tough time with algebra. When I learn the concepts of algebra that I don't understand right now, I'll get better grades. I'm going to keep working on it."

By being more positive and not putting myself down, I actually help myself do better. I like it when other people encourage me. So it only makes sense that I encourage me, too.

I've learned that what people call positive thinking and positive self-talk is like giving yourself a paint job. Why be a "just me" when I can be a "great guy"? Why be a lousy student, when I can be a student who just has a little trouble with algebra?

I'm glad that my girlfriend made the comment she did

because it helped me understand a simple equation: Just as I sign the letters I write to her, "Love, Dan," I can sign thoughts to myself that way, too. When I write "Love, Dan" to her, it's intended to let her know that my feelings for her are positive and loving, so why not make my own thoughts and words to myself as positive and loving as possible, too?

I think the words we use are like a coat of paint. So, be sure you choose the "right" color!

Dan Belana, 17

2

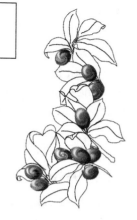

You Can . . .
If You Think
You Can

*If think you can or if you think you can't,
you're right either way.*

—Henry Ford

FERRARI, ANYONE?

A young boy came home crying from school one day. His grandfather was visiting and greeted him.

"Why are you crying?" his grandfather asked.

"Because Paul called me a sissy! Do you think I'm a sissy, Grandpa?"

"Oh no," said his grandfather. "I think you're a Ferrari."

"A *car*?" said the boy, trying to make sense of what his grandfather had said.

"Well, if you believe that just because Paul called you a sissy that you really are one, you might as well believe you're a car, and a terrific one at that," explained the grandfather, asking, "Why be a sissy when you can be a Ferrari?"

"Oh! That's cool, Grandpa!" the boy exclaimed, now realizing that he got to have a say in how he felt about himself.

"Yes, it is," replied his grandfather. "The opinion you have of yourself should not only count as much as anyone's—but even more."

A Word from the Authors

Self-worth—what we think about ourselves—shows up in the things we say and do. We may even misinterpret the words and actions of others because of the view we hold of ourselves. The boy's grandfather knows how important it is that his grandson see himself as having great value—in this case, seeing himself as a "Ferrari" instead of a sissy. It's important to see ourselves in the most positive light that we can. Seeing the good in ourselves helps us to do better, to "be" better. We all have days when almost everything about our lives looks bleak. On those days, it's easy to feel bad about ourselves. Looking on the bright side of things can help us transform tough times: "Just because I'm having a difficult time in one subject doesn't mean that I'm not a good student," or, "Even though the girl I want to date won't go out with me, that doesn't mean I'm not a likable, lovable person."

The good news is, psychologists tell us that we are hurt less by the calamities of life than we are by how we see them. And this is never more true than when applied to how we see ourselves. Not only do we have the choice to paint the events and situations in our lives in the color that we choose, we also have the choice to paint *ourselves* in the color we choose. In other words, you get to choose whether the cup is half-full or half-empty when it comes to how you see yourself!

Like the grandfather in the story above, the many teens we heard from also know how important it is to cast a positive vote when it comes to their own self-worth, saying that self-esteem and actions went hand-in-hand. From becoming a better athlete, to getting better grades; from being a friend, to attracting better friends; from getting along with your parents, to being granted more privileges, self-esteem plays a big role. Jennifer Jones's story of Sergio—her sister's boyfriend—received your first-place vote for being an example of a Ferrari, even if her father wasn't all that happy about Jennifer's sister wanting to marry him. Thirteen-year-old BeShawn Niles explains why his stepfather is a first-class Ferrari—in spite of the name-calling BeShawn's step-dad suffers at the hands of BeShawn's father. He admires that his stepfather is self-confident and doesn't allow anyone else's opinion of him to be more important to him than his own self-image. And Sam Rollins, fifteen, tells us why he thinks being a Ferrari means being *his* best—not necessarily being *the* best. Fourteen-year-old Noreen Nicoles said if she was "so smart," the good grades she gets would come easier for her. When her dad tells her she shouldn't be so tough on herself, Noreen decides at least she's willing to try seeing herself as a Ferrari—and said she'll keep us posted as to whether it works. And your ninety-year-old friend Elmer Adrian pondered what another person with the "same frame, background and foibles would have done with his life—if it had been theirs instead of his!"

If you deserve an A, why settle for a B? When his teacher let him grade his own paper, seventeen-year-old Paul Drexler had a chance to think about that question. He concluded as did the rest of you: Seeing your value means treating yourself accordingly. After all, you wouldn't enter your Ferrari in a demolition derby!

A Ferrari Without an Engine

Last semester, after we had turned in our final class project in our biology class, the teacher told us to assign ourselves a grade based on how well we felt we had done on the project. My buddy, Reese, gave himself an A. He really did do a great job on the project, and probably it was an A project.

I knew my project was even better than his. After completing a unit on mollusks, our class was supposed to do a report of our choosing related to the subject. Reese did his report on the New Zealand Paua, a mollusk with a blue-green iridescent colored shell that's often used in costume jewelry, like in the ring his little sister had. He wrote up his report, and then when he presented it to the class, he showed them his eight-year-old sister's ring.

I decided to do my report on the differences between a natural and cultured pearl. The more I got into reading and researching the pearl, the more interested I became. I really put my heart into the project. I found out that the formation of a pearl is actually the result of an irritant, such as a grain of sand, that has gotten into the shell of the oyster. In order to protect itself from whatever is invading it, whether it's a piece of sand or something that feeds on this sort of mollusk, the oyster secretes a white liquid substance to protect itself. It will encrust anything within its reach. Sometimes when a natural pearl is cut in half, a grain of sand or some small creature is found inside of it.

I was surprised to learn that a pearl's size can vary from between that of a pinhead to that of a pigeon's egg. The Hope Pearl, which is the largest pearl ever found, is nearly two inches long! The Hope Pearl is kept in the South Kensington Museum in London. So, for my report, I wrote the museum and asked for information on the Hope Pearl. They sent me a lot of material, including some really great photographs, which I included in the report. Everyone, especially the teacher, was impressed. This made me feel pretty good because I really put a lot of time and work into my project—and it showed. It was a great report.

I knew that the project I handed in was A quality. Reese's report was good, but mine was much more complex than his. Even so I gave myself a B. And you know what, the teacher gave my friend Reese an A and gave me a B! I think that says a lot about the value we place on ourselves. There was no reason for me to devalue the amount of work and time I had put in on this project to make sure it was excellent. I'm not saying that Reese overvalued his paper, but if his was worth an A, for sure mine was worth one, too! But I didn't stand up for myself and the quality of my work on the project.

It was a good lesson for me. I'm making an effort to be more honest in presenting my own worth. It's obvious that my buddy Reese considers himself a Ferrari. And while I would never want to give myself an A when I don't deserve it, I don't want to give myself a B when I deserve an A, either. I know my report was a Ferrari of a report! But it didn't get the A it deserved because its engine stalled—that engine being the confidence I had in myself. If I had considered myself the Ferrari that I am, rather than a Ferrari without an engine, I would have given myself the grade I deserved.

Paul Drexler, 17

Sergio

My sister is dating a really great guy. His name is Sergio, and he's a fireman.

Sergio is definitely a Ferrari.

My sister and Sergio are pretty serious, and I think she'll probably end up marrying him. This really bugs my father, who tells my sister that she can do better than a fireman.

I think my father is being unfair, first of all because it is my sister who has to live with Sergio, not my father. Second, Sergio is one of the nicest people I know. He's polite and considerate to everyone, especially my sister. He takes her to nice restaurants, to concerts and to almost every special event in the community.

I think being a fireman is an honorable profession, even though my father says it's not much of a "lifestyle." And I can understand Sergio's wanting to be a fireman. When he was a small boy, his family's home caught on fire late one night. The family was already asleep. Luckily, the fire department arrived within minutes. The house was quickly engulfed with flames. Though Sergio's mother tried to rescue her two small children from their bedroom, she was overcome by smoke inhalation. Firemen then rescued each member of the family.

Sergio remembers being carried out of the house by a particular fireman, one who kept in touch with Sergio's family over the years. To Sergio, the men who rescued his family and carried him from the terrible fire are heroes. That fireman is the reason they are all alive. Sergio really admires firefighters. And why not? They literally saved his brother and mother's lives. His, too.

How can you say that someone who uses his life in such a purposeful way is not as good or worthy as an executive like my father, who makes a lot of money in his job, but doesn't particularly like the people he works with (he's always complaining about them)? Sergio's work, on the other hand, makes him feel important and needed by others. He loves what he's doing and is happy with his life overall. And he constantly works to improve himself. Though he's already graduated from college, he's taking more courses, especially classes about saving lives.

My father said it must be boring being a fireman because of all the "down time on your hands." I don't see it that way at all. Firemen do a lot more than wait around for a fire to happen. From the things that Sergio and my sister tell me about his work, I think it must be interesting. He meets a lot of people and he gets to travel—even out of state. Just last month when a huge forest fire broke out, Sergio was called in to help. When it was all over, Sergio was credited with saving the lives of nearly three hundred wild mustangs and other wildlife!

Regardless of what my father thinks of my sister's boyfriend, I think when Sergio looks at himself in the mirror, he genuinely likes and respects who he sees. I know I really admire him. And I think my sister would be wise to marry someone who is proud and pleased with who he is. Sergio is the kind of guy I'd like to have for a friend—and as a brother-in-law. I'm very happy my sister is with him.

When a person genuinely is comfortable with who he is, it shows. I think Sergio is the kind of person we should all strive to be like.

Jennifer Jones, 16

Every Time a Cute Girl Walked By . . .

I broke up with my girlfriend, Allison, because every time a cute girl walked by, Allison started ragging on her, saying how dumb she was, or criticizing the way the girl looked or what she was wearing. At first it didn't bother me because I told myself I was with a girl who was "cool"—and better than the other girls. But then I realized that what Allison was saying wasn't always true. Some of the girls she put down as dumb were not at all dumb, and they looked just fine to me.

At first, I thought Allison was just jealous of the other girls. But then I asked myself, "Why should Allison be jealous if she believes she's prettier, smarter and dresses nicer than they do?" I came to the conclusion that Allison's habit of putting others down didn't really have anything to do with the other girls. Allison just didn't feel good about *herself*. She didn't see herself as a Ferrari.

I think Allison thought that if she found something wrong with other people, it made her look better. She made others seem "less" so she could be "more." I really "got it" about Allison at our last Talent Day. Sometimes you don't know how talented your friends are, but at Talent Day students get to share their talents with everyone in the school. Some of the kids sing or play musical instruments, other kids get together and perform a skit. They really get into it, making costumes and props. Talent Day is supposed to be fun, and I think it is. It's a day to display another dimension of yourself. It's great!

At our school's last Talent Day, everyone was laughing, cheering and clapping for a friend who was on stage. Everyone was having a great time—in the audience and on the stage—all except Allison, who for some reason felt it was her place to act as the event's critic. As though she expected a Broadway performance, Allison judged and criticized each person. As usual, she was especially critical of the girls, most especially the really popular or cute ones.

There I was enjoying myself and my friends, having a good time, while my girlfriend—sitting right beside me—seemed grouchy about the whole thing. I wasn't sure what to do. You're supposed to feel loyal to your girlfriend, right? I mean, I'm supposed to like her personality and the things she says and does.

On that particular Talent Day, I realized that I disliked more things about her than I liked. Even though Allison is pretty and smart, it didn't make up for her jealousy and put-downs of others. I began to feel bad about myself for being with Allison. I broke up with Allison that day.

Since then, Allison has had two different boyfriends. (She's not with anyone right now.) Maybe they've discovered what I did. It's not really all that much fun to be with someone who continually puts everyone down.

I think that when you bad-mouth other people, it's a sign that you don't feel all that secure about yourself. I've decided that no matter how cool you are (or think you are), when you tear others down, it takes away from your image of being "cool"—from being a Ferrari.

For people who put others down, think of this: In the end, you're going to find yourself alone, like Allison.

Shawn Hamilton, 16

Something's Always Wrong With . . .

I used to have a friend named Toni, who always found something wrong with other people, even strangers. She'd say things like, "Look at those hideous shoes that woman is wearing. You'd think she'd have enough sense not to leave the house in them!" Or, "Can you believe he's wearing that ugly old shirt with those pants? He must not have any mirrors in his house." Or, "Look at her big butt. I'll bet she weighs three hundred pounds. She ought to get her mouth wired shut."

Another thing Toni always did was gossip, even when someone told her something in strict confidence. It never mattered to her if what she said might hurt someone's feelings. "Tommy told me not to tell anyone, but he says Brad's thinking of breaking up with his girlfriend Kathleen," she said to me as we were standing in the lunch line, with Kathleen in earshot. Kathleen heard her, just as Toni knew she would. Kathleen was very upset and started crying. Toni acted like she'd had no part in hurting Kathleen's feelings. Toni has a really strong personality.

Another bad habit of hers was criticizing other people openly and humiliating them in front of other people. She did that to Mr. Sams, our history teacher. Mr. Sams has a really long nose. Toni drew a picture of him—complete with a cartoon-like exaggeration of his nose—and hung it on the bulletin board. She'd sketched his desk beside him with his nameplate sitting on it, so everyone would know it was Mr. Sams. Beneath it she wrote, "If you filled your nose with nickels, you could afford to get a nose job."

I thought Toni was pretty funny until I was on the other end of her habit of criticizing people. But now I see it was because she didn't feel like a Ferrari.

One day, I asked Toni if she wanted to go with me to watch my little sister's softball game. When the team took their seats on the bleachers in front of us, Toni pointed to a little girl wearing braces and thick glasses and said, "That girl is so ugly, she'd have to play in an open school team, because she couldn't find anyone in her neighborhood to play with her. In fact," Toni added, "she's so ugly, I bet her mother has to tie pork chops around her neck to get the dogs to play with her!"

That little girl with the braces and thick glasses was my sister!

I was very upset, and decided Toni had gone too far. But it did teach me a lesson. Toni's mean comment made me realize that when she was making fun of people I didn't know, I thought it was funny, and it all seemed harmless. But when a demeaning comment was directed at my sister, it sounded especially cruel. When people say things like that about strangers or people you know, they're mean-spirited—period. People who feel really good about themselves don't get satisfaction out of hurting others.

And I learned another lesson, as well. My mother told me that if someone is comfortable with talking about others, then she's probably not going to hesitate to talk about you, too. My mother was right. Even though I thought Toni and I were the best of friends, it got back to me that she had made a comment about me behind my back—one that was not very flattering.

When Toni turned her "put-downs" on me, I got a chance to feel the effects. It was not a good feeling. For sure, it didn't make me feel like a Ferrari.

Rita Sultanyan, 14

Because I'm So Smart

Kids always tell me that I get good grades *because* I'm natu-rally smart. I don't see it that way at all. I mean, if I am so smart then I wouldn't have to work so hard at getting good grades—which I do.

Good grades don't come easy for me. *If* I were smarter, getting good grades would be so much *easier*.

My dad says I shouldn't be so tough on myself. He says that if I encouraged myself instead of putting myself down, then get-ting good grades would be easier for me.

I have a history exam coming up and I want to do well on it. My dad says I should see myself doing well and say positive things to myself like, "I'm going to get a good grade on the exam. I've read the chapters; I've studied; I know the material." I think basically what he's telling me is to see myself as a Ferrari.

I'll keep you posted if my dad's theory works.

Noreen Nicoles, 14

One "Hot" Ferrari

My father really dislikes my stepfather, Mike, and is always calling him names, saying what a "good-for-nothing" guy he is.

Mike knows about his name-calling because sometimes when my father comes to pick me up, he'll say inconsiderate things right in front of my stepdad like, "Is *what's-his-name* going to pick you up after the game, or am I supposed to bring you home?"

Even though it's rude that my father doesn't call Mike by his name, my stepdad doesn't hold it against my father. "Sure, I'll pick up BeShawn at 3:30," he'll answer. Nor does Mike make a big deal about my father's inconsiderate attitude towards him. He lets the comments go.

I asked my stepfather if the way my father treats him bothers or upsets him. "Oh, not really," he said. "You don't always have to be right, as long you do what's right." I like it that Mike is secure with himself. My father's taunts don't bother Mike because he likes himself. My dad's opinion of my stepdad doesn't change the way Mike feels about himself.

I really admire Mike. I especially like how he's good to my mother. And I really like what a good father he is to me. I appreciate all the things he does for me, like teaching me to throw a fastball and helping me with my homework—without becoming impatient like my father does. Mike even volunteered at my school's carnival this year. No other stepdads were there.

Though I would never tell my real father that I think my stepfather is one of nicest guys I know, he is. I'm happy to have Mike as my stepfather. Sometimes, I even call Mike "Dad" because he acts like a dad to me. In my eyes, my stepfather is a really great guy—one hot Ferrari.

BeShawn Niles, 13

Part 2

Friendship: Finding, Keeping and– Sometimes–Losing It

A friend is someone with whom I can reveal many parts of me, even those I am meeting for the first time.

—Jennifer Leigh Youngs

3

Good Friends Are a Necessity of Life

ELEPHANTS AND FRIENDS HAVE A LOT IN COMMON

When an elephant is ill or injured, other elephants in the herd gather around to protect the animal, and to bolster it up. They know how important their support is because if an elephant in such a condition lays down, it won't be able to stand up again on its own. So, the other members of the herd literally surround the weak elephant and help it remain standing. Even when on the move, the other elephants walk next to the ailing elephant, supporting it as they travel.

Just as elephants intuitively know when one of their friends needs assistance, they also know when that friend no longer needs support, and so, they gradually give the elephant a little more room until it walks and functions on its own.

A Word from the Authors

Amazing, isn't it? Animals, like people, intuitively know when one of their friends needs their help. A good friend is someone we can count on, as well as being so much more. A friend is someone with whom we can relax and just hang out, have fun and share our innermost thoughts—deep dark secrets, lofty and noble goals, or our hopes, joys and fears. A good friend allows you a safe space to share your deepest thoughts and needs—without worry of being judged, criticized or made to feel silly for feeling the way you do. Friends cheer each other on, laugh and cry together, and just plain commiserate and listen to each other. That's *why* friends are *friends*.

A good friend helps you become a better, wiser and more compassionate person than you might have been without that friend in your life. Friends help us grow into being who we are or, as Jennifer said, "A friend is someone with whom I can reveal many parts of me, even those I am meeting for the first time." What a wonderful gift, a real taste berry.

As you'll see from the teens you'll meet in this chapter, it's crystal clear that teens sincerely value their friends, and can speak eloquently about the important role their friends play in their lives. From coping with the death of a loved one (which so many teens had experienced), to dealing with the everyday ups and downs of life—like sharing a secret too good to keep, or mourning a breakup with a special someone—teens agree that friends are *very* important.

Making no secret of the fact that they treasure the support they receive from each other, teens shared openly about the sense of connection and strength they gain in knowing their friends will be there to understand and support them. Seventeen-year-old Roma Kipling's friends gathered around when she lost her beloved grandmother. For Roma, it was a friend—as much as the love and support from her family—who helped her through a painful experience. Experiences as painful as the loss of a loved one stir up a lot of deep feelings—everything from doubt and anger to guilt, grief and depression. Many of these feelings can be difficult to handle. Because they are emotionally painful, these feelings can even lead to physical illness if not dealt with in a healthy manner. While friends are there for us when we walk through the heartache and grief of the death of a loved one, sometimes we need even more support. Should you be going through such a difficult time, we urge you to seek the support of your family, as well as the counseling you need to process your grief. As we discussed in part 1, many schools offer peer crisis counseling, which can provide you with crucial support. If your school doesn't offer these services, you can turn to an adult you trust—whether it's a parent, teacher, school counselor or clergyman—to help you find the counseling you need.

A friend came to the rescue of fifteen-year-old Susan Hinkle when she found herself the only member of the group unwilling to leave a private party at a pizza parlor to "go look up some guys," while seventeen-year-old Bradley Dawson's best friend is the first person he looks for the moment he leaves the locker room after a game—especially if he's played poorly. Barbara Allen, thirteen, describes how completely different her friends Kayla and Sara are from each other. Though Kayla's support can border on insulting, and Sara won't always give her honest opinion, Barbara explains why both are really good friends.

Yes, friends are important as they help each other along the road of life, especially *real* friends. Sixteen-year-old poet Peggy Nunziata tells us how to know *for sure* if a friendship is "real."

Enjoy their stories!

Our Friendship Is Real

I'm sitting here thinking about the past,
Hoping in the future our friendship will last.
We have been friends for a short period of time,
And been through a lot, even so, we're just fine.

I've seen lots of people come and go,
Saying and doing whatever—careless, you know?
That's why your friendship means so much to me,
When I'm with you, I feel secure, whole, and so free.

Free from those who won't be around,
When times get tough, and I am down.
You'll be there for me and understand how I feel,
Because we both know our friendship is real.

Peggy Nunziata, 16

For You to Cry In

My grandmother was one of my very favorite people in all the world. Her name was Tilly, but I called her "Grams." She liked that.

Grams was so much fun to be around. She lived in a small apartment about forty-five minutes away from my family. She visited us often, and we visited her quite a bit, too. She lived her life to the fullest, and was always very involved in each one of ours. Just this past summer, she took me with her on vacation, a vacation she planned with just the two of us in mind. It was a vacation for, as Grams told everyone, "Just us two girls." We went to Washington, D.C., for eight days. While we were there, we went to the White House and the Lincoln Memorial. We visited museums Grams said I had to know about, and other "places of interest." And we got to eat dinner in a restaurant every single night. It was so much fun!

Grams had a way of making everything exciting. One night we went to a theater to see an opera. Everyone was dressed up, really dressed up, like in tuxedos and long gowns. Grams and I dressed up, too. We even had our hair styled at a salon. In my opinion, the opera itself wasn't all that great, but being with Grams sure was. And she was right when she said it was fun to "appreciate the ambience." Everybody at the opera was so cool!

Besides being fun to be around, Grams was one of the most positive people I've known. She had a way of making me feel like I was truly special. She believed in me and felt I could do anything I wanted, and that I would. She told everyone that I was "destined to grow up and change the world." She'd tell everyone she introduced me to, "My granddaughter is going to become a very important person, you just watch and see. Someday she'll be president of the United States, or maybe she'll just create the cure for all diseases—or the formula to make everyone in the world happy and forever young!"

She was like that. With her, I was an "unlimited" person.

But then, when she was only sixty-one years old, Grams died. I had visited her only two days before. She seemed healthy and was her usual, happy self. Mom said she died from a brain aneurysm.

When it happened, I was heartsick.

Knowing how much I loved and missed my grandmother, my two best friends pretty much did what the herd of elephants did for their sick friend: They rallied around me. Their parents allowed them to stay home from school and go with me to my grandmother's funeral, a gesture I hadn't expected. And the days following my grandmother's death they were so extra kind and sensitive to my feelings. Regularly they asked, "Are you doing okay?" or "Are you feeling better?" I found that so loving, and it showed me that they understood the hurt I was feeling.

The evening after the funeral, both of them came to my house. They brought me a stuffed animal with a note: "For you to cry in." They both stayed over that night, which was really nice. We just hung out, doing things like rearranging my closet, playing CDs and just talking.

My friends' empathy toward my sadness was like a big comforting pillow. They really cared and understood. It was so consoling, and it gave me a sense of friendship that I hadn't really felt from friends before. For sure, my friends helped ease the pain I felt over Grams's death.

Since that time, our friendship has been solid, and we're tighter than ever—inseparable really. We share everything. We help each other through the tough times—like being grounded, failing an important test, not being asked to a big dance and painful breakups with guys we were certain we were going to be in love with forever. And we help each other with the important things—like getting dressed to go out on a big date (a team effort), and planning what to wear to school when something big is going on and we want to look extra-great, like for class pictures or a school assembly. We trade clothes, fashion and makeup tips or model a potential outfit and exchange brutally honest opinions about what looks best and where and why something doesn't work. Because we are such good friends, we can do this without misunderstandings and hurt feelings.

I will always miss Grams. She was such a good friend; it showed in everything she did. I think it's possible to take friends for granted, and to think that friends are friends no matter what—which is not necessarily so. It doesn't just happen. More than anyone else, it was Grams's "style" of friendship that helps me understand that a friendship is special because of the things that people do to make it special. The relationship between my grandmother and me was special because Grams made a point of making it special—like my friends and I do for each other.

We laugh together, cry together, cheer each other on and commiserate and listen to each other. Like the elephants, we gather around to help each other. And because we do, we each know we can count on the other—in good times and in bad.

Roma Kipling, 17

A Bad Day for the Rest of the Day

Some parents think that their own kids like and need their friends more than they do their parents. It's not true. When I'm in an argument with my mom or dad, I have a bad day for the rest of the day. It's not like I can have an argument with my parents and then go to school and just forget about it. It's very upsetting. If my parents and I have had an argument, I can be sitting in class, but I'm not really paying attention to what's going on because I'm off in my mind, still thinking about the argument.

Rather than concentrating on what the teacher is saying, I'm still involved: *What* were my parents thinking? *Why* did they say what they did (or didn't)? Then I wonder why *I* said what I did—or why I didn't say what I should have! And then I try to decide on a good time and a good way to reopen a conversation with them so I can go where I wanted—or get what I wanted or have what I wanted—in the first place!

So I sit in class, planning a new strategy, and playing through every possible response—several times. Which means, of course, that I'm still not paying attention to what's going on in my class. This upsets me too, so then I get worked up all over again.

I'm sure I'm not the only one this happens to. My friends feel equally upset when it happens to them. So, even though it's really important to me to feel close to my friends, it means even more to me to feel close to my parents. Like me, most of my friends respect their parents, and want to have a good relationship with them. I think a good friendship with your parents is like the elephants' scenario, where they all help each other. When my parents and I are seeing eye-to-eye, a lot of things in my life look okay to me.

Megan Burres, 16

Most Valuable Player

I've discovered that being around someone who believes you're a terrific person makes you feel that you *are* a terrific person. And because of that, you automatically want that person for a friend.

The person who sees and brings out the best in me is Chad Diamant. People say that Chad is a "really together guy," and I can see why: He feels really secure within himself and makes others feel more confident, too. Chad has a special knack for seeing the "up" side of life. To him, the glass is never half-empty. It's always half-full. A good example is when I play in a football game. If I do well, he has no problem congratulating me on a good game and making me feel like a hero. And if I have a really bad game, in which I play really poorly, he doesn't focus on that. Instead, he points out some of the good aspects of my playing, like how I helped another team member to score or make a good play. He turns it around so that once again I end up looking like the most valuable player.

Even if our team lost, he won't dwell on the loss. Instead, he'll talk about some aspect of the game or particular plays that were especially good. "Lousy game," I'll say.

"No way!" he'll counter, and then say something like, "You were great in the third quarter! I saw the way you blocked that pass. The team's very lucky to have you!" With Chad I can't lose: I'm an MVP every game.

Because of Chad's support and positive attitude, he's the first guy I look for when I come out of the locker room. I consider him the most valuable friend I have, a real MVP in the game of life.

Bradley Dawson, 17

I Keep My Earplugs Handy

Sometimes you don't think about your parents as being friends, but they can be. Mine are.

My dream is to be a professional musician. I'd like to be a real star. Sometimes when I tell that to some of my school-friends, especially those who don't know me all that well, they look at me and give a little laugh, like they don't know how to take it. You know . . . am I a serious talent or am I an egotistical jerk? My parents don't laugh or question me. And they didn't doubt that I could learn to play a saxophone. They bought me one last year.

I didn't realize a saxophone was so hard to learn!

I know I must have made a lot of racket as I tried to play it, but my mom and dad never complained. "Sounds great!" Dad tells me. "You're really getting good!" Mom says. Four months ago, I had just about decided it was too much for me to master, but both Mom and Dad assured me that they had no doubts I could do it. So I didn't give up. I can't wait to be a rich and famous sax player. Like my Dad says, "You can do anything you set your mind on." I love how my parents support *me* just like the elephants support one another.

So, when I do make it as a professional, I'll owe a lot of my success to my parents for buying me my saxophone of course, but also for believing in me. So until then, I just picture myself up there on stage with the bright lights. And in the front row I see my two best friends—my mom and dad—with their little black shades on, clapping their hands, smiling.

Oh yeah! I'll make 'em proud! I just need to keep practicing. And my earplugs handy.

Jeremiah White, 17

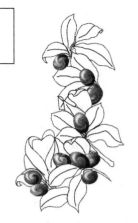

4

The "Rules" for Being a Friend

DID I PASS YOUR TEST FOR FRIENDS?

I try to read your eyes,
surmise,
just what you think behind that brow.
As you nod,
are you thinking that I am odd?

You seem not to be impressed
at what you see;
I am
a nonentity?
You're in a hurry to forget,
What made me second-class?
I see I didn't pass the standards you have set
for friends.

Our story ends.

Elmer Adrian, 90

A Word from the Authors

As much as friends are friends, they still have to pass the standards you set for friendship—being able to talk openly and honestly is one of them. As your friend, Elmer Adrian, said, if you can't talk openly, the "story ends."

Many of the teens we heard from said that they *expected* their friends to acknowledge them when they did something especially good—like aced an exam, or played well in a tournament or looked extra good. That a friend is able to give you feedback about these things is more than just a matter of praise. It encourages and inspires you to continue to do your best. Being able to express yourself is an important thing between friends. We urge you to reach out to friends and family. As so many of the stories in this book show, teens can be a good source of help and understanding. Remember, many schools offer peer counseling programs, in addition to programs staffed by professionals trained to help teens and sympathetic to their needs—both can be extremely helpful. Most important, just remember you are never alone—there are people who care and who can help if you reach out to them.

Good communication is not always easy, as Belinda Carr, sixteen, points out, but it has its benefits—as sixteen-year-old Beth Brown discovered: "being allowed to spend time with my friends means knowing how to communicate with my parents!"

"You know, Mom, expressing yourself, saying what's on your mind and in your heart is so important. Caring enough to show compassion and empathy for what others are going through is what endears us to others and shows our humanness. But, an often overlooked fact of good communication skills is that they are primarily based on good *listening* skills. If you watch closely, you'll notice that the best-liked and most popular kids spend as much time listening to others as they do talking. I think being a good listener is one of the most ignored aspects of making and keeping friends, and of getting along with others in general.

"Good listening means you are really paying attention. Everybody knows someone who pretends to listen, but really only listens with 'half an ear,' continually interrupts, acts bored or shows indifference to what you're saying. It doesn't feel good to have someone do this to you. In fact, it makes you feel unimportant, inferior and generally insignificant. After all, this person has made it pretty clear that you had nothing interesting to say. When I was a senior in high school, a teacher did an experiment that clearly pointed out how unnerving this is. It was a day when we each were to give an oral report in front of the class. Trent— a really popular and well-liked student—was called to the counselor's office in the middle of his presentation. This was a set-up, but Trent didn't know it. When he left the room, the teacher instructed us to be 'an obnoxious audience.' Some of us were to lay our heads down on our desks, others were to gaze out the window and still others were to pretend to scowl or shake their heads in disagreement. When Trent returned to the classroom and continued his presentation, we went into our 'awful listeners' mode. After only a few minutes of speaking, a very frustrated Trent stopped and asked, 'What is going on? Why are you treating me this way?'

"It just goes to show you that listening is an attitude. We must *want* to listen and not just wait for our turn to talk. We need to give our full attention when our friends are talking. Don't comb your hair or fidget with your jewelry when someone is talking to you. Look at that person, show your interest, suspend all judgment and just *listen*. Don't play with the rubber bands on your braces or look around to see if anyone you know is nearby. Let the person who is speaking finish before you say anything. This shows that you care enough to listen and that you respect the person enough to care about what she has to say. It also gives you time to think about what the person is saying and an opportunity to gather your thoughts and decide how to respond. Try it and you'll be amazed at how much it improves your friend-ships—and all your interactions with people—and even increas-es your popularity with others."

"It's a good point, Jennifer. Listening is only one of the skills of effective communication, but it is a very important one—espe-cially with your friends.

"Of course another good communication skill in friendship is being kind and treating friends as you would want to be treated. Being kind shows that you are a happy person who likes herself and other people, that you are open to getting to know people better, and that you are considerate and thoughtful."

"Don't forget the boomerang, Mom."

"The boomerang?"

"Yes. My friends and I always say, 'Remember the boomerang!' Basically, it means, 'Don't send out what you don't want to come back.' Like a boomerang, the things we do and say—both good and bad—usually come back to us sooner or later. If you say something inconsiderate about someone, your words will act as an immediate payback—you'll feel ashamed of yourself for being inconsiderate and cruel. Everything you send out boomerangs back to you. If you project an attitude of gratitude, it comes back. If you project happiness and goodwill, cheerfulness and consid-eration, these, too, return. If you gossip, it'll come back to haunt you, too, as I'm sure Mia in the story 'My Friend, the Thief' will find out! You receive what you give. If you can remember that one phrase, you can help yourself be kinder and nicer to others—a 'taste berry'!"

The Secret She Kept

For almost the entire school year, I liked a boy named Ben. I was pretty sure he didn't know. I never told him. Besides my mom, the only other person who knew was MaryAnn Drew, and I'd sworn her to secrecy! I didn't tell anyone else because it might get back to Ben. What if he didn't feel the same way? I was too shy to take the chance he might feel differently than I did.

"Asking Ben to the Sadie Hawkins dance?" Mom asked.

"I'd love to; I just don't have the nerve," I told her.

"Hmmm," she said, and then told me a story about "two very close friends" of hers when she was in school.

Katie liked a boy named Sean. But she never told him, forever keeping the secret to herself. When she saw him sitting at the other end of the lunch table, or with friends, she couldn't help but admire the way he listened intently to his friends, and always seemed so considerate and attentive.

Eventually both Sean and Katie began to date—but not each other. On so many occasions, Katie secretly wished her date was Sean, rather than who she was with—but it was her date, and not Sean, who asked her out. The night of her senior prom was especially bittersweet. When a favorite song of hers by Anne Murray was played (a song that always made her think about Sean), she looked to Sean, dancing with his date. Sean was looking in Katie's direction. They smiled at each other, their smiles lingering. For the entire evening, Katie gazed at Sean dancing with his girlfriend, Annie Pauls. Annie was so outgoing, Katie just knew she'd never stand a chance, even if she did get up the nerve to talk to Sean. But that didn't keep her from looking and dreaming—and wishing it was her dancing in Sean's arms.

After graduating from high school, both Katie and Sean went away to college in different states. But Katie never stopped missing him.

Both Katie and Sean attended their five-year high school reunion. When the band began to play, both Katie and Sean found themselves standing alone, each looking for a dance partner. Many of their classmates were married and were there with their spouses—but neither Katie nor Sean had married.

Katie looked at Sean across the room, and though butterflies took flight in her stomach, she walked over to Sean and asked him to dance.

"You're even more beautiful than you were in high school!" Sean whispered to her as they were dancing.

"Oh," she accused, "in high school, you didn't even know I existed."

"On the contrary," Sean corrected, "you were the love of my life. I was just too afraid to tell you. There wasn't an event that went by that I didn't wish you were my girl. You were so beautiful, so bright—and so reserved—I just knew you wouldn't go out with me. I decided I would rather secretly believe that you loved me than to have my Katie turn me down. Our senior prom was the worst. I kept looking at you, wishing you were my date. There was one song, one special song that just broke my heart. It was 'Can I Have This Dance, for the Rest of My Life,' by Anne . . ."

". . . Murray," Katie said, finishing his sentence for him.

"Yes," said Sean. "Do you know it?"

"Yes," was all she said.

My mother knows the story very well—you see, my mother's name is Katie. And Sean is my father. Later that long-ago evening, he asked the band to play "their song," and that's when he asked her to marry him.

It's a great love story. Even though this story ended happily, it's bittersweet, too, because my parents missed out on all those special times in high school when they wanted to share things with the other. They could have been "boyfriend and girlfriend" for all those years.

My mother's story gave me the courage to ask Ben to the Sadie Hawkins dance at school. He said yes! I doubt "our story" is going to end up like my parents' romance did, but I'm having a great time!

Stephanie Cohen, 16

Party On!

Five of my friends and I had gathered at our favorite pizza place for our friend Nicole's birthday party. We were all having a good time, talking and laughing, when all of a sudden, Michelle said, "Hey, I've got a great idea! Let's go to my house, call some guys I know, and party on!"

"I'm not sure that's a good idea," I said. I looked to the others for support, but it looked to me like the other girls were considering going. Either that or they didn't know how to say "no" to Michelle. Michelle always tries to bully the rest of us. Michelle knew that we'd all get in trouble with our parents if we left the pizza place, but that didn't keep her from pressuring us to go. So I reminded her that Nicole's mother had said, "Under no circumstance are you girls to leave before I get here!" I knew she'd heard the words as clearly as I had. "She's bringing Nicole's birthday cake at 8:30," I said. "We can't just not be here when she arrives!"

"So what?" Michelle said, like it was no big deal if Nicole's mother showed up with the cake and we weren't there. I thought it would be pretty rude if Nicole's mother came with the cake and we were gone. Plus, I knew my mother wouldn't give me permission to go to Michelle's house. In fact, she'd be furious if I left without getting permission. So I suggested that we should wait until *after* Nicole's mom had arrived with the cake. Michelle just laughed, and said, "Oh, stop being such a dweeb. Let's go. She'll find us!"

Four of the other girls, including Nicole, started to get up to leave. I couldn't believe my dilemma. "Hey, I'd like to go, too," I said, standing my ground, "but I just can't. My mother is expecting to pick me up here in an hour."

"Call her and tell her to pick you up at my house instead!" Michelle said in a really sarcastic tone of voice.

"She and my father went to dinner someplace, and I don't know where they went!" I lied, not really wanting to tell her that I knew my mother would say "no."

"Suit yourself," Michelle said. "The rest of us are going."

"You guys, it's really not a good idea—think about it," I pleaded. Then Michelle started swearing at me, calling me names worse than "dweeb." I felt tears coming to my eyes, so I ran to the bathroom.

I felt so childish, standing in the bathroom, crying alone, while my friends were getting ready to do something more exciting. But I knew it wasn't right to leave the pizza place. It's really hard to go against your friends, especially when you're hoping to be more popular with them. I was standing in the bathroom wondering how long I was going to stay there, assuming they'd all left, when Amanda came in. "I'm sorry that Michelle is being so mean to you," she said, trying to comfort me. "She's just that way. I agree with you that we shouldn't leave. I mean, Nicole's mother is expecting to find us here, and she's even bringing a cake. And besides, I'll get into trouble with my parents if I leave and go to Michelle's house, so I'd better stay here, too."

"Did the other girls leave?" I asked.

"No," she said, "not yet. But I think they may. But if we get out there right now, maybe we can convince Tammy and Ellie to stay—and Nicole, too."

"Okay," I said, feeling a little bit relieved. I dried my eyes, and we left the bathroom.

"I'm staying here with Susan," Amanda announced as soon as we returned to the table. Then she said something I hadn't expected. "If I leave I'll get in trouble with my parents, too, so I think we should take Susan's advice and just stay here."

Nicole looked relieved as she blurted, "I'll stay with you guys. My mom would ground me until my next birthday if I just took off when she told me not to."

"Okay, I'll stay, too," Tammy said, shrugging her shoulders.

"Me, too," Ellie added.

"Well, I'm not going alone! I'll stay, too. Geez! What wimps!" Michelle griped.

"Better wimps than grounded," Amanda said.

I was so surprised it was that simple. None of the girls left, and I know it was because Amanda sided with me.

Not only did Amanda's siding with me make me feel better, but she was also the deciding factor in the other girls staying, too. Even though the two other girls had seemed willing to go along with Michelle, it only took the two of us to convince them to stay.

I guess it's true what they say: There is strength in numbers. Friends can influence each other. For good and bad. "Alrighty, then," I said, feeling like a victor. "Party on!"

Susan Shrinkle, 15

"Cooler" Than You Think

When I was in junior high, Kent wasn't exactly the most popular guy in school. Actually, he was sort of a nerd. Hardly anyone talked to him—not for any particular reason, just nobody said much to him.

One day, after getting my lunch, I looked around for my friends in the cafeteria. They weren't there yet, and it was kind of crowded, so I took the first open seat I saw. I found myself sitting next to Kent. We started talking.

As it turns out, he's not so "different." In fact, Kent is a pretty smart guy. He's just quiet.

I was surprised to learn that he collects sports cards like I do. He even has a Ken Griffey Jr. rookie card—which is worth a couple hundred dollars—that he got from a three-dollar pack of cards! What luck! And, for his birthday this year, his uncle gave him a game-worn jersey card (that's one of the really cool cards that come with a small piece of the athlete's jersey right on the card). We had a really good conversation about where to find some good deals on some of the rare and hard-to-find cards. Kent told me he has both "Tough Stuff" and "Beckett" card books, which are the best ones to tell you what every card is worth. While we were talking, we found out that we each have a couple of cards that the other wants. So now we're going to get together to compare our cards. To tell you the truth, I'm really looking forward to getting together with him. He knows all about which ones are really hot and which ones are supposed to be going up in value. It's totally cool.

It just goes to show that sometimes people who are not popular might be cooler than you think. If I hadn't taken the time to talk to him, I would've missed out not only on knowing all those things about sports cards, but also on knowing a really cool guy.

When my friends saw me with Kent they teased me about it

later. When I told them about what we had talked about and that he was an interesting and pretty neat guy, they didn't say much. But now when my friends see Kent, they talk with him. And they treat him like a regular guy.

All because I sat with him for a few minutes that day in the lunchroom and found out that he definitely passed my test for being a friend.

Carl Galloway, 14

If You *Really* Want to Know

Kayla and Sara are both friends of mine, but they're very different. For instance, the other day the three of us were going to go to the movies. "Do I look okay?" I asked Sara.

Without even so much as looking at me, she replied, "Yeah, sure. You always look great."

"How about my hair?"

"Yeah. Looks great," she responded.

The moment Kayla walked in, she took one look at me and demanded, "You're not going to be seen in that, are you? No way am I going to be seen with you if you wear that!"

"What's wrong with it?" I asked.

"Well, for one thing, you look like a little kid in it, and for another, there's a mustard stain on the left sleeve." She paused, frowned and then added, "Having a bad hair day?"

So you can see how different they are. Sara is a person who doesn't want to upset you, so she always says something nice and would never want to make you feel uneasy, no matter what. Kayla is very blunt and outspoken. She has very definite opinions and isn't afraid to be honest. Kayla is definitely not afraid of what you'll think about what she has to say. So if I really really want to know how I look, while I ask them both, it's Kayla's advice that's worth the most. She has no problem telling me her honest opinion about anything. If the way I look passes her inspection, I can be sure that it will pass with others. Now, if I was worried about a big test at school, I'd go to Sara for help. Kayla puts as little energy as possible into her grades. Sara, on the other hand, is very smart, understands what it's like to want to get good grades, and will help you out when you need it. So both Kayla and Sara are good friends, each in her own way.

Friends. They're so different. That's why you need lots of them.

Barbara Allen, 14

So I Threw His Letter Back at Him

I remember the night my boyfriend and I broke up. We went to a movie, and on the way home I mentioned that I was planning to get a new dress for the big school dance that was coming up. I asked him what he thought he was going to wear. That's when he told me he couldn't take me to the dance. That really upset me. And frustrated me. I really, really liked him, but I often found myself without a date for many of the special things going on. If he was my boyfriend, my *only* boyfriend, why wouldn't he want to take me to all the many things going on?

By the time we reached my house, I was even more upset. Thinking that we wouldn't be going to the big dance upset me so much that I didn't even wait for him to finish what he was saying. I got out of the car, and as I was slamming the door, I hollered, "Well, fine, if you don't take me, then I don't want to go out anymore. We're through!"

Later that night, he called and asked, "Can we talk?"

"No!" I yelled and hung up.

The next day at school he walked over to me while I was at my locker and tried handing me a note. I was still mad, so I grabbed the note and threw it back at him. Looking sad, he just walked away.

I picked up the note so none of the other kids who saw it when it fell to the floor would read it, stubbornly tossed it in my history book—where it stayed on the top shelf of my locker for the next several days. I was just miserable.

Sitting at home—the night after the dance—I took my history book from my backpack, retrieved his letter and read it.

Dear Connie,

I'm sorry I can't take you to all the things that I'd like to. I'd love to take you everywhere—to every dance, every movie, to the fair when it comes to town, to restaurants. I don't know how to tell you this and still be fair to you, but it's just that most of the money I earn from my part-time job goes to help my mother pay our bills. She works hard to take care of me and my brother and sister, but she just doesn't make enough money to do it alone. I love being with you. . . . going places and doing all the little things that make you happy. . . . I just can't afford to right now.

I miss you. . . . you know that we should be together. . . . I know how important it is to you to go to the school dance. If you don't mind that I don't rent a tux, if you don't mind that the corsage I give you isn't made of the orchids I know you deserve, then I'd love to take you to the dance. I miss you so much. Please reconsider.

Love,

Kurt

Now whenever I hear about good communication skills, my heart aches because of the way I treated Kurt. He is such a good guy and I really hurt him—all because I refused to listen. The irony is that because I wouldn't communicate, I ended up hurting myself, too. I'm a better listener now and I don't jump to conclusions so fast. That's been helpful, too! And, I now read love notes the instant I receive them!

Connie Hunt, 16

Part 3

The Right Stuff: Attitudes for Life Success—Becoming a Person of . . .

Success in life isn't a given—it costs attitude, ambition and acceptance.

—Jennifer Leigh Youngs

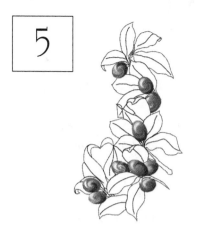

5

A Person
of . . .
Integrity

The truth of the matter is that you always know
the right thing to do.
The hard part is doing it.

—Gen. H. Norman Schwarzkopf

EQUAL PAY FOR EQUAL WORTH

One day my father hired three young men to help him put up the hay crop. At the end of the day he gathered them around to pay them.

"What do I owe you, John?" my dad asked the first young man he had hired.

"Fifty-five dollars, Mr. Burres," John said. Dad wrote him a check for fifty-five dollars. "Thank you for your work, John," my father said respectfully.

"What do I owe you, Michael?" my father asked the second young man who had worked the same number of hours as John.

"You owe me seventy-five dollars," Michael said.

With a look of surprise, my dad asked quietly, "How do you figure that, Michael?"

"Oh," said Michael, "I charge from the time I get into my car to drive to the job site, until the time I get back home, plus gas mileage and meal allowance."

"Meal allowance—even if we provide the meals?"

"Yup," replied Michael.

"I see," said my dad, writing him a check for the seventy-five dollars he requested.

"And what about you, Nathan?" Dad inquired. "What do I owe you?"

"You owe me thirty-eight dollars and fifty cents, Mr. Burres," Nathan said.

Again my father was surprised at the discrepancy in the amount requested. The third young man, like the other two, had been hired for the same job and had put in equal time (and had come from the same small town just a couple of miles away). My father asked for clarification.

"And how did you arrive at that figure, Nathan?"

"Well," said Nathan, "I didn't charge you for the lunch break since your wife prepared and served lunch. I didn't have gas expenses since I came with my buddies. So the actual number of hours worked brings my pay to thirty-eight dollars and fifty cents."

My father wrote him out a check for one hundred dollars.

Dad then looked at the three young men—stricken silent by my father's actions—all of whom were a bit bewildered by the differing amounts on their individual checks.

"I always pay a man his worth, boys. Where I come from we call that equal pay for equal worth." He looked benevolently at the three young men before him and in his typical fatherly style added, "The values in a man create the value of a man."

Bettie B. Youngs
Excerpted from Values from the Heartland

A Word from the Authors

Integrity is being right with yourself—no secrets, no hidden agenda, no dishonesty, just "what you see is what you get." A friend of ours, author and management consultant Dr. Ken Blanchard, put it this way, "There is no pillow as soft as a clear conscience." What's true about integrity is that even if someone else is upset with you, or doesn't agree with you, or doesn't think you did the right thing, if you know in your heart of hearts that you did, their opinion matters less. What they say or think is—in a way—beside the point.

Even though Nathan saw that my father was willing to pay the guys the sum each asked for, his integrity won out, and he treated my father with fairness—and reaped the rewards in return!

"Mom, Nathan's not the only one who has learned a thing or two about the rewards of integrity! When I was in the tenth grade, my friend Sherri always called me while she was doing homework. Then, because she developed a regular pattern of not finishing her homework—and started to bring home low grades—her parents told her she couldn't talk on the phone until she'd finished her homework. They felt it interrupted her concentration. Sherri thought this rule was really unfair and told them that talking on the phone with her friends didn't have anything to do with whether she finished her homework. So her parents made a deal with her: if she earned good grades that semester, she would be allowed to use the phone while doing her homework. Unfortunately, even though Sherri wasn't allowed to call any of her friends that semester, she still received low grades. So, on the day when she knew her report card would appear in the mailbox, Sherri rushed home and took the mail before her parents did so they wouldn't see her report card!"

"Why are you laughing, Jen? That's not funny!"

"Oh, Mom, it is and you know it, but I will admit it's not

honest. Besides, the report card was addressed to her parents, not to her. Her trying to conceal her grades and opening her parents' mail was wrong. But, the good news is she knew it and eventually did the right thing."

"*Eventually?* Something tells me there's more to the story."

"Well, Sherri didn't really know what to do after that. She didn't have any real plan other than 'just don't let the parents see it.' Plus, she has a really good relationship with her parents, and she knew that what she did wasn't right and she felt bad about it. So, she asked a couple of her friends—including me—what she should do. Our friend Carl told her that eventually her parents would start to wonder where her report card was. He suggested that she change the low grades to higher ones and then give her parents the report card. He even showed her how to do it."

"Jennifer, I'm disappointed—"

"Mom, you know Sherri would never have gone as far as changing the grades on her report card. She really wanted to be honest with her parents—it's just that some things are hard to give up, like talking on the phone with your friends whenever you want. Sherri did give her parents the report card and she told them the truth. She did it because she felt bad about having done something dishonest and she didn't want to continue doing one wrong thing after another. She did it because she is a person of integrity."

Jen's eyes sparkled with the affection and appreciation we hold for good friends, as she added, "I'll never forget seeing Sherri at school the next day. I asked her, 'Why didn't you call me last night?' She answered, 'I told my parents everything that happened and I promised to bring my grades up, so I have a lot of work to do in a couple of my classes. But don't worry—next semester I'm going to get great grades. No one can afford to go without talking to her friends on the phone!'"

As Sherri found out, the good feeling of doing the right thing is the greatest reward of integrity. As the stories in this chapter show, teens have a lot of their own experiences in coming to know the value of integrity. Wanting money for a special date, sixteen-year-old Mark Truitt charged for services "not yet rendered," and found he was "no longer needed." Sixteen-year-old Connie Gedding learned a similar lesson when she "snuck" out the back door at work, once, and then twice . . . until she finally got caught. "Integrity," she learned, "is earned."

While integrity may have to do with what other people think of you, it also has to do with what you think of yourself. Many of you realized that integrity is doing what's right even if no one else is looking. No one else was looking when Tomoko Ogata, fifteen, found someone else's money—money no one knew was missing. As teens said, being a "taste berry" means being true to what you know is right—even if you know no one else is looking. Why? Because what you know to be true about yourself is as important as what others think of you. That's being a "taste berry!"

The "Advance"

My savings account is just about zeroed out right now, since I just paid my car insurance. So, I needed to earn some extra money so I could afford to rent a dinner jacket and buy the tickets to a special dinner-dance I wanted to take my girlfriend to.

One of the ways I make money is by doing yard work in my neighborhood. Since I needed the money right away, the next time I worked for one of my neighbors, Jim Thomas, I told him that I had done some extra things—like trimming, hedging, weeding, stuff like that—and charged him for it. Only I fudged on the amount of time I told him I had worked, thinking that I'd make the time up over the next couple of weekends. Mr. Thomas didn't doubt my word, and paid me for the hours I said I worked. I was pretty happy to have the money "in advance."

The next day I got a call from Mr. Thomas. He said it was time his eleven-year-old son "took over the yard duties" and that he didn't need my services any longer. I think Mr. Thomas took the yard job away from me because I had stretched the truth—and he knew it. I felt really terrible I wouldn't be able to give Mr. Thomas the extra work that he'd already paid for "next time." There'd be no "next time" now.

I know that if I had been honest with Mr. Thomas, he would have loaned me the money I needed. Just last summer, when I went to a special two-week soccer camp, he asked me if I needed some extra money to take along. I wish I hadn't taken advantage of him. I think that whenever you take advantage of someone you may think you get away with it, but in the end you usually don't. It's bad enough that I lost a good job, but I also lost Mr. Thomas's trust and respect. And I feel bad about myself for having done it.

From here on out, I'm going to practice honesty in all the things I do.

Mark Truitt, 16

I Have to Live with Myself and So . . .

I have to live with myself and so,
I want to be fit for myself to know.
I want to be able as the days go by,
Always to look myself straight in the eye.
I don't want to stand with the setting sun,
And dislike myself for the things I've done.
I can never hide myself from me,
I see what others may never see.
I know what others may never know,
I can never fool myself and so . . .
Whatever happens I want to be,
Self-respecting and conscience free!

Excerpted from I CAN Ignite the Community Spirit
by Joy J. Golliver and Ruth Hayes-Arista

These Grades Are for You

When I was in seventh grade it was really important to me to earn good grades—to make my father happy. With each report card I took home, I'd sit there eagerly waiting for his smile and praise because I'd gotten good grades. Mostly I got As and Bs. Then one semester I got a D, so I said to my Dad, "I can't believe the teacher gave me a D."

"No," my Dad corrected. "Your teacher didn't give you a D. You earned a D. Nor did your teachers give you these three As and a B. You earned them, just like you earned your D. If you need more help in a course because it's difficult for you, I'll do what I can to help you. But in the end, I want you to do the work and set the standard for the grade you want as something you're earning for you—not for me."

I think my dad made two really good points. First, he was right; my teachers weren't *giving* me a grade, I was *earning* a grade. And second, I should earn that grade for myself, not for my dad. I'm learning to take responsibility for the grades I "earn," and to see them as something I want for myself. I still want to please my father, I can't see that ever changing completely, but I'm the one who sets the standards for what I want for myself. I'm the one I have to please, at least first.

And it's my dad who taught me this. It showed me that he trusted me to set standards for myself. I think that's what integrity is all about: Trusting yourself to be honest—with you. After all, if you can be honest with yourself, you will automatically be honest with others.

Jason Samuels, 16

I Lost a Fast Twenty Bucks

Several months ago while standing in the check-out line at the grocery store, I saw a twenty dollar bill fall from a lady's purse as she took a check from her wallet. No one even noticed the money float to the floor. I was standing behind her waiting to pay for a bag of M & M's—my regular three o'clock pick-me-up. I leaned over, tucked the cash into my hand and tightened my shoelaces. It was so tempting to pretend the only reason I'd bent down was to tie my shoes. I wanted to go to the fair with my friends on Saturday, and my parents had told me they weren't footing the bill, that I'd have to take care of it myself. I didn't have the money to go to the fair. I looked down at the bill in my hand, thinking that it sure would be handy to have that money! I thought about it—for about three seconds. I knew I had to give her the money back. The woman was very grateful.

If I had taken the money, even though no else might have found out, I would know. Then I'd have to think about how I had stolen it and live with feeling bad about doing it. There are more advantages to being a good person than there are in trying to "put one over" on someone. Even if no one else finds out that you are an honest person, at least *you* know you are.

I know I felt better about myself because I gave the money back to her.

I have integrity—with me.

Tomoko Ogata, 15

I Got Caught Cheating

I thought the worst thing about science class was checking on the growth of mold samples we made from old beans, bread, bananas and other "hairy" food. Whew, what a smell! That was, until my science midterm at the end of the semester. My father knew how important it was that I do well on my science test. So he helped me study, and the day of the test he even fixed me breakfast. Then, he gave me one of his "you can do it!" speeches.

Even with his help, I wasn't all that confident that I'd ace the exam. Since my dad had helped me, I didn't want to let him down by getting a low grade. Then, I made a really bad decision. To tell the truth, at the time it felt less like a decision and more like an impulse.

Anyway, I got caught cheating.

The school called my dad and told him what happened, and they scheduled a parent-teacher conference (with the vice-principal!). Needless to say, my dad and I talked. He explained that failing isn't bad; it's just an outcome, and not a final one. I was really glad that he understood—although he said it would be the last of his "good-guy understanding." He said that he'd tolerate a failed exam now and then, but not cheating. "While failing can mean a lack of preparedness," my dad went on, "cheating can never mean anything other than a lack of integrity." I got the message. And I learned something else: When you cheat, you usually doubt yourself and your ability to master what you've studied. The whole incident, including my father's disappointment in me, taught me something I never would've guessed—I'd rather fail a test honestly, than pass one at the price of cheating. It just isn't worth the way it makes you feel.

Les Williamson, 16

6

A Person of . . . Determination

Great dancers are not great because of their technique; they are great because of their passion.

—Martha Graham

ARISTOTLE

One day a young man came to Aristotle, the great philosopher, and begged, "Please, Aristotle, I want to learn all the knowledge you possess. Teach me all you know!" to which Aristotle answered, "I'll consider your request. But first let us go for a walk down by the river."

The young man followed Aristotle to the riverbank. Once there, Aristotle picked up a stone and dropped it into the water. "Retrieve the stone," directed Aristotle. As the young man stooped over to pick up the stone, Aristotle dunked the lad's head under the water and held it there until the boy began to swing his arms and squirm for freedom. He needed to breathe and was intent on getting the air he needed.

Discerning the lesson was learned, Aristotle released his hold on the young man. Gasping, the young man heaved in great gulps of air, and once he caught his breath demanded, "What did you do that for?"

Aristotle said simply, "I will give you and teach you all that I know, but it will do you no good unless you want it badly enough—unless you want it as much as you wanted air to breathe."

A Word from the Authors

In his attempts to create an electric light, Thomas Edison tried and tried and tried before he finally succeeded. After many failed attempts, a critic said to him, "Edison, you should give up. You've failed thousands of times."

"No, I haven't failed thousands of times," Edison retorted. "On the contrary, I have successfully eliminated thousands of ideas that do not work!" So remember, don't ever give up!

Just recently, we attended a very special gathering for a group of dynamic and successful people. Gathered together for the purpose of camaraderie and sharing their stories of success were some 350 guests, the likes of physics Nobel laureate, Jim Cronin; Emmy-winning producer of NBC *Nightime News*, Roberta Oster; Charles Bailyn, an astronomy professor who discovered a "black hole"; producer Ralph Winter of Walt Disney Productions; Phil Lader, the U.S. ambassador to England; New York civil court judge, Dorothy Chin Brandt; Bill Broyles, screenwriter for "Apollo 13"; former U.S. diplomat and Harvard physics professor and now president of Queens College, Allen Sessoms; Steve Smith, a veteran of two space flights, over three hundred Earth orbits and three space walks; Bill Perry, U.S. Secretary of Defense—you get the idea.

When you bring together a group of supremely accomplished individuals such as these, you can only imagine the number of stories of success they can tell! We were in awe. But heroes and leaders rarely sugarcoat their successes. If you listen closely while they tell of their route to a gold medal, a peace prize, an invention or discovery, or for an office they were seeking, you learn an interesting truth: Rarely, if ever, did that person succeed on the first try! Most all successful men and women can cite an example or two (or more!) of the times they did not succeed. And each will tell you not to discount or dismiss these failures, but instead to use the failure as an important lesson and feedback to go forward. In other words, the information they glean from what doesn't work becomes as important as information about what does work. Many said that it was a "mistake" or "failure" that led them to an important finding and resulted in new information that led to a new discovery or invention or successful outcome.

What would these accomplished people want you and I to learn from them? First, that almost everything worth doing takes a lot of effort. Second, a failed attempt is as good a reason as any to try again, and this time, incorporate what you have learned in the process!

That's what seventeen-year-old Mark Whitman learned (albeit with a nudge from his father) when an unexpected loss at a state finals wrestling match forced him to rethink "failure." It wasn't until his fifth try that Steve Smith qualified to become an astronaut! His advice? "Just as in learning to walk or ride a bike, you keep learning until you don't fall down anymore. Set your goals high and never give in. And never, never, never give up!"

So when a challenge seems insurmountable, or you feel discouraged, think of Edison! What if he had given up because one or more of his attempts did not meet with success? Probably, someone else with more fortitude and stick-to-itiveness would have looked at the progress Edison had made, including reviewing the "failed attempts" to see what had already been tried but didn't work, and then, using all that Edison had already accomplished, gone on to invent the electric light!

To paraphrase Aristotle, "You have to want it bad enough!"

Steve Smith's Dream

As a young boy, Steve Smith was fascinated with the mysteries of space and dreamed of one day becoming an astronaut. When he was in the third grade, he drew a picture of a rocket ship. The picture was so dear to him that he hung it where he could look at it daily. He loved the picture because it coincided with his dream, one in which he saw himself as an astronaut, one who would someday walk on the moon!

Steve held onto his dream over the years. While still a young boy, he read everything he could that was related to space and space travel. He learned everything he could about the National Aeronautics and Space Administration (NASA). By the time he became an adult, only one thing remained: earning a coveted position as an astronaut on NASA's prestigious space team. And so he began the rigorous and arduous training program, a prerequisite in qualifying to become an astronaut.

The day for which Steve had so carefully planned and trained finally arrived. Today was the day when all those who had aspirations to be an astronaut would be put to the test.

Within a few days, NASA announced who had made the team. Steve had failed to make the cut!

As disappointed as Steve was, he was determined to succeed. According to NASA's regulations, a person is eligible to go through NASA's training only once every two years. So, two years later, Steve tried again.

Once again, he failed to make the cut.

So he tried again two years later!

Once again, he failed to make the cut.

So he tried again two years later!

Once again, he failed to make the cut.

So he tried again two years later. On his fifth try, Steve Smith became an astronaut on the United States of America's NASA team!

Today, astronaut Steve Smith is a veteran of two space flights, over three hundred Earth orbits and three space walks! His advice? "Just as in learning to walk or ride a bike, you keep learning until you don't fall down anymore. Set your goals high and never give in. And never, never, never give up!"

Bettie B. Youngs

[**Authors' Note:** *This drawing is the actual picture of the rocket Steve Smith drew as a third-grader! He asked us to please include it for you. Just imagine how this simple picture gave birth to a noble dream. Through hard work and great determination, Steve Smith made that dream reality. He is now a respected astronaut and an American hero.*]

Favored to Win

Success is not measured by your victories,
but by your recovery from your failures.

—Vic Preisser

Last year my wrestling team made it to the state finals. Of all the contenders, I had the best record and was favored to win. Everyone was counting on me to win—and winning was necessary to advance to the nationals.

No one wanted to win more than I did, but I lost my match! It was such a shock and disappointment to me.

I felt defeated in more ways than just on the mat. For several weeks afterwards, I couldn't seem to get back into the stride of things. I lost interest in working as hard as I had to get good grades and do well in school. I even lost interest in the extracurricular activities I was involved in, and that surprised me because I had been enjoying them before, most especially the photography club. I spent time alone instead of hanging out with friends after school. Everything seemed so pointless, so bleak. I felt really depressed.

My father was the one who helped me pull myself from the fog I was in. He helped me turn things around. He told me that, yes, my having an opportunity to attend the national competition would have been a great honor; and, yes, winning there could have opened up other doors (like being selected to work as a junior coach at special wrestling camps, or getting a college scholarship); and, yes, "It's okay to think about what happened, to understand what kept you from the outcome you had hoped for, but after a review, it's time to focus on your achievements and move on, to recover, to rebuild." Then he said something I'll always remember: "Son, a loss is just a loss, and not your finest achievement. Don't give it so much power. Save your time and energy for the next endeavor. Focus on that. Your finest achievement always lies ahead."

My father helped me realize that failing at some things is going to be a given, and that losing at some things is the flip side of winning at some things. I found his perspective and advice helpful.

I love my dad for believing in me and for trusting in my ability—win or lose. He gave me the push to keep on being determined to succeed—not to give up, but to continue moving towards success. I just hope that one day I can become as inspirational to others and to my own kids, when I have them, as my father is to me.

Mark Whitman, 17

Part 4

Deciding What to Do in Life: Discovering Your Interests, Talents and Direction

*The goal is to make your joys your job,
your toys your tools.*

—Jennifer Leigh Youngs

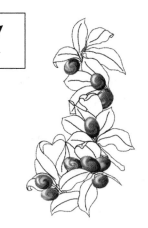

Finding Your Acres of Diamonds

The world makes way for the person
who knows where they are going.

—Ralph W. Emerson

ACRE OF DIAMONDS

An Arkansas farmer, tired of not being able to make a good living on his farm, sold it to a man who had very little money, and went off to seek his fortune elsewhere. Several years passed and still he had not found the fortune he sought. Tired, and now broke, he returned to the community of the farmstead he sold. One day, he drove by the farm he once owned—the one on which he could not make a living. To his surprise and amazement, the farmhouse had been torn down and a mansion now stood in its place. Several new buildings including a large barn, a huge machine shed and a grain dryer and storage unit had been erected. Rows of trees and shrubs had been planted. Beautiful lawns adorned the meticulously groomed grounds. The place had changed so much that he could hardly believe it was the same farm. He decided to stop and have a talk with the new owner. "Look at all you've done," he remarked, clearly bewildered by what he saw. "How on earth did you accomplish all this? You barely had enough money to buy the farm from me. How did you get so rich?"

The new owner smiled and said, "I owe it all to you. There were diamonds on this property, acres and acres of diamonds!"

"Diamonds!" scoffed the previous owner. "I knew every inch of this land, and there were no diamonds here."

"On the contrary," responded the new owner as he pulled a lump of what looked like an oily piece of quartz from his pocket. "I carry around this small nugget as a good luck charm."

The farmer was amazed. "That's a diamond? I remember seeing a lot of those all over this land, so many that I was frustrated thinking what rotten luck it was to have owned a land filled with hard rock formations—so many that it made plowing and planting difficult!"

"Well, it's obvious you don't recognize a diamond when you see one," commented the farmer. "Diamonds in their unpolished form look like lumps of coal."

A Word from the Authors

Finding your acre of diamonds—discovering what interests you—is an important first step in deciding what you'll do for work. The big questions are how do you discover it and how do you know when you have found it? The farmer sold his acre of land, certain there was nothing of value on it. Some of the teens we heard from felt the same way, certain that they didn't have any special talents that they could turn into a job or career. Upon closer examination, they discovered they did.

"Mom, seventeen-year-old Trent Dayton told us, 'I have a passion for the ocean,' and then explained *why* he loves to go surfing. Trent said that some people called him a 'surf bum' and didn't see him as having big goals or plans for his future. 'You can't make a living being a surfer!' a classmate in Trent's careers class jeered. In careers class, the students discussed the issue of turning their passions into a living. Trent and his jeering classmate, Bruce, had very different opinions and very different passions. Bruce planned to be an attorney. This was his dream and he had his college plans and the goal of owning his own law firm set before him. Right after Bruce made his statement about Trent, the teacher held up his hands and said, 'Wait, I wouldn't be so sure of that.' Another classmate volunteered, 'Trent could surf professionally.' 'I'd like that,' Trent conceded, 'but it's not my dream.' Then, with the teacher's prodding, the class learned that Trent did have very real goals and dreams for the future. They are based on his love for the ocean and it's very possible for him to make a living doing what he loves.

"Trent's dream is to own his own surf shop and to manufacture his own surfboards. Trent has already developed great skill at shaping surfboards and he knows all there is to know about what a surfboard shop needs to carry—quite impressive accomplishments for someone his age. Add his knowledge and skills to his passion for the ocean and for surfing, and you have a large arrow pointing to the entrance of a diamond mine. With just a little unearthing, Trent and his classmates discovered that his goals and dreams were as clear and as possible to achieve as Bruce's were. Learning that Bruce planned to go into business law, Trent was a good enough sport about Bruce's earlier razzing to joke with him, saying, 'Maybe someday I'll hire you to draw up some contracts for me.'"

"Jennifer, that's a great example of discovering that your interests and talents have everything to do with pointing you in the direction of 'making your joys your job,' as you say. Now that Trent has identified his passions and thought about what he'd like to do, he'll be better able to decide what further education and training he needs to give wings to his goals."

"I think that's why so many teens we heard from said, 'Teenagers often have very good ideas about what they want out of life. Some people may think teens are clueless or mindless about these things but they aren't. They just get frustrated when others aren't listening to their ideas, dreams, goals and plans.'"

As you'll see in the stories in this chapter, when teens looked closely at the things going on in their lives, they found diamonds. As a struggling, teenage mother determined to finish high school, Julie Newman, seventeen, found the diamond of her future career. And Julie's not playing around—she's determined to give Mattel Toys some serious competition! An encounter with orphans in Bogotá, Colombia, helped sixteen-year-old Lisa Cartwright refuse to be seen as a "loser" anymore. Finding an injured cat and taking it to the vet crystallized seventeen-year-old Kevin Tulane's love for animals. Having found his "lucky" acre of diamonds, Kevin now knows he wants to be a vet. As a result, he's become a better student, developed better relationships with his parents and brothers, and even with his classmates. In Kevin's own words, "Knowing what I want to do has made all the difference. For the first time in my life, I feel on track. Dreams fill my mind. My heart suddenly has goals that are worth doing. Now I'm energized."

Many teens felt as if they stumbled upon their diamonds by chance. Seventeen-year-old Richard Lewis described his newly found passion for film production as a "gift in disguise"—and tells Steven Spielberg to move over! And fifteen-year-old Mark Knolls tells us why his brother's not being able to afford to take his car to the auto repair shop may help that same brother own his own auto repair shop someday.

It can take time and honest introspection to come to know yourself well enough to be certain of what you want to do. Until you reach that point, it's important not to become discouraged—and to keep looking for those answers.

Luckily there are definite places to look. Just as Brent Lasorda took a class, so can you. Brent's class was a summer course at a junior college, but often high schools offer classes that help teens discover potential career skills by identifying strengths and aptitudes. Your own high school may offer just such a class. If you follow the community calendar section in your local newspaper, you can find out about career-day events in your area. During these types of events professionals in a variety of careers set up booths to offer you information on the kind of work they do. It can be helpful to learn more about what tasks different professionals perform and what different positions and career options are available. You can also meet with your school guidance counselor or school career counselor. These counselors are trained specifically to help you find ways to discover where your talents lie. We live in a world of computers, so take advantage of this resource, too. Ask your counselor about Web sites and software programs that can help you in your search. In addition, there is a wealth of books (including workbooks) that can walk you through nearly every possible phase of figuring out what to do in life. Your school and community libraries should carry these books. Ask your librarian to help you locate them.

A part-time job can help you clarify your interests and talents, too. Look carefully at those things you like and dislike about your job. If you dislike stocking shelves but love waiting on customers, that's a good indication that you'd like a career working with people. On the other hand, if you just love spending your work hours entering data and dislike having to answer phones, you'd probably be happier in a job where you don't directly deal with people. One teen worked in a clothing store, and while she didn't like working the cash register or assisting customers, she discovered she loved window design. This led her to pursue a career as an interior designer. The goal is to find what you love to do—whether it's because you're great at it, or it gives you a sense of purpose or you just think it's fun. Usually, when you find it, it will involve all of these.

In the following stories, teens search for their "diamonds." Let's join them on their search!

A Pain in the Butt

In his acceptance speech for winning an Academy Award for his performance in a motion picture, Oscar-winner Robin Williams thanked a number of people, including some high school teachers. "Some of my teachers thought I was 'a pain in the butt,'" he laughed, referring to himself as jokester, a funny-bone who could always see the humor in things as a teenager. And then, clutching his Oscar and growing serious, one of America's most beloved comics remarked for all the world to hear (perhaps attributing some of his success to her), "but one special teacher said to me, 'I hope you'll channel that talent. You'd make a good public speaker!'"

Obviously the teacher saw great possibility in Robin's sense of humor. How forturnate we are that the teacher encouraged him to do something with it: It was to be the start of something very special. As his Academy Award confirms, the "pain in the butt" turned a very spectacular piece of coal into a brilliant diamond!

And of course, that Mr. Williams acknowledged the teacher is the mark of a winner, a real "taste berry!" [1997 Academy Awards telecast interview.]

Bettie B. Youngs

The Incredible Six

Last summer, I took an eight-week course at a local junior college. The course was all about discovering what's called our aptitudes—our "acres of diamonds." The instructor told the class that we can tell a lot about our aptitudes—the things that we're naturally interested in—if we pay attention to the times when we're doing something and it really captures our attention. He said we'd know when that was because the time would just fly by.

One of our assignments was to keep a journal for eight weeks. The teacher told us to keep track of the books and magazine articles we read, and the movies or television programs we watched. Using a six-point checklist, we had to write about each one, telling what it was about the book, article or show that we either liked or didn't like. He also gave us other assignments to help us discover the kind of things we were interested in.

I learned a lot more about my interests—my deeper interests—because of it. The moment you've finished reading a book, or if you've just come out of a movie, right away you know if you liked it or not. And you intuitively know that there are some you prefer over some others. The bigger question is, "Do you know why?" Before I took the course, my criteria for whether or not I liked a book was whether it bored me or if I fell asleep reading it. And if you asked me to review the book—whether I liked it or didn't like it—before I took this class, I probably would have said, "It was just boring." That would have been my response.

Now, I would answer you with a little more insight and be more specific. Now I might say something like (as I did recently in a book report), "I didn't enjoy it because the setting for the story took place nearly five decades ago and in a foreign country, and I couldn't relate." Or, I might say that it was precisely because of those things that I loved the book.

Another point in the checklist asked us to watch for specific detail. If I were applying this to the book I'd read, I might ask, "What is the nature of the story?" For example, does a human-interest story grab my attention more than a story about animals? If my answer is "yes," then according to the teacher's checklist, the next thing I might explore is to see if I'm caught up in the adventure of how the person's dilemma is going to be resolved, or am I most interested in how the person himself is going to change as a result of the ordeal? Things like that. The checklist we were given helped us examine a lot of different things, all aimed at finding out what we were *really* interested in.

One of the last items on the checklist was to see if we could spot the interests of others, and if we could, to describe what we saw. So I used my friend Kirk as a "guinea pig." One weekend, he and I went to the Wild Animal Park—a place I love no matter how many times I go. I watched Kirk glance from one animal to the next, only occasionally amused or interested by what he saw. I couldn't help but compare it to the way I felt when he showed me all the "great" stuff that he could do on the computer. There'd be moments where I thought it was really cool, but for the most part it bored me. Kirk obviously felt this way about animals.

Though I still don't know exactly what career I want for sure, I think the method I learned in the summer-school class will be very valuable in helping me determine my "acre of diamonds."

Brent Lasorda, 17

Because He Couldn't Afford a Car

My seventeen-year-old brother really wanted a car, but my dad said a car was something my brother and I had to get on our own ("so we'd appreciate it")—so there would be no help from my parents with buying one. Although my brother found a part-time job, he was also playing sports, and it didn't leave many hours for his job. I remember my brother telling me that he felt like he'd be out of high school by the time he saved up enough to buy his own car. But then, knowing my brother couldn't afford a car, when my uncle bought a new car, he offered my brother his old one—but it needed a lot of repairs.

Since my brother didn't have the money to spend for someone else to fix it, and because he didn't know how to do it himself, he took a shop class to learn how. Not only did he get good grades in shop, he thought the class was fun. The few hours he was working in his part-time job were enough to pay for the parts he needed, and before long his car was up and running.

One thing led to another, and soon other kids were asking my brother for help with their cars. He even did a few repairs on my dad's car. Then, the shop teacher convinced my brother that he should take other classes that would teach him how to run a successful business, like an auto repair shop. Right now my brother works at the school's auto repair shop.

I have no doubt that one day he'll have his own auto shop—and all because he didn't have enough money to take his car to one!

Mark Knolls, 15

A Gift in Disguise

I really wanted a certain part in the spring play our high school drama club was putting on. I knew I'd be great in the part because I'd been in plays for the last three years and really like acting. Plus, it's such an honor to get selected for a good role and all. I've even thought about being an actor.

Well, I didn't get the part. The teacher asked each of us to help with the lighting and sound, as well as with other behind-the-scenes roles. Two of my buddies were so upset at not being chosen for the lead role that they said no to the behind-the-scenes work. I have to admit, it was my first thought, too, because I was disappointed I wasn't getting chosen for the part. At first I figured, well, I'll just wait and try out for the next play—which was only three months away. But then I decided, why not learn all you can about the theater? It might come in handy to know this stuff.

Boy, did I find out how true that was! Not only did I learn that I was really good at production and behind-the-scenes work, I also found out I enjoyed it. What I didn't know was that I would enjoy it even more than acting! Now I'm certain that I want to be a film producer. Move over, Steven Spielberg!

As it turned out, it was really good that I didn't get chosen for the part. I'm happy that I agreed to work backstage. It was a gift in disguise—because I've discovered my acre of diamonds.

Richard Lewis, 17

College Is My Next Destination

When my cousin Alex, who is already a college graduate, asked me what college I planned to go to, I said, "To tell the truth, I'm not sure what kind of career I want, so how can I know what college I want to go to? Why should I even go to college?"

"Go to college," Alex said firmly. "Believe me, it gives you four more years to think about what you want to do and that can be helpful because sometimes it's hard to know what you want to be when you're still in your teens. It'll give you time to get it all figured out—and besides, except for studying, college is *great* fun!"

Alex gave me some great suggestions. First, he told me to go talk to my guidance counselor at school. It turned out she had all sorts of information for me. Once I started looking into colleges, I began to get a lot of different literature with information on all sorts of different schools. I received brochures, applications and other information from colleges all over the country.

Next, Alex told me that I should go visit all the schools I was most interested in attending. Through my guidance counselor, I found out that my high school even offers a tour of four of the major universities in my home state, so I signed up for it. Alex said if my school didn't offer the tour, I could have called the admissions office at each of the universities and asked to arrange tours that way. Most universities offer tours and orientations for potential applicants during spring break, but Alex said it's even better to see the schools during their regular day-to-day operations—that way you can walk around, check things out, sit in on classes and ask yourself whether you'd be happy going to school there.

I also learned about books that rank colleges. You can find them in any library reference section. They rank each school academically, financially and by certain majors—some books even describe campus life. When I went to check out these books, I found another book that shows which colleges to attend and which subjects to study if you want to make a difference in the world. That book really gave me a lot to think about. Now, I'm looking into becoming an environmentalist.

For my birthday, Alex gave me a great gift: a software program that helps you choose the right college! There are lots of different software programs designed specifically for that purpose. Mine gives me information—good, brief overviews—on sixteen hundred four-year colleges and universities. It prompts me with questions and my answers create my own personal profile. Then, I can rank and categorize my own college preferences. All this will help later when I have to answer questions on the college applications. After using the program, I realize that college is the best choice for me. I'm also learning tips for coping with dorm life, writing application essays, getting letters of recommendation and qualifying for financial assistance.

I'm glad I'm lucky enough to have Alex for a cousin. He really pushed me in the right direction. Every time he sees me, he asks how I'm doing and what progress I'm making. "Going to college is one of life's most important road trips," he always tells me, "so it takes a lot of thought and research. But don't let the stress of all those major decisions take the fun out of planning for it! In the end, it's the adventure of a lifetime—make sure you have fun as you mark your destination."

I still don't know my exact career destination, but I do know I'm going to go to college. Now I see college as an important step toward choosing a career. And, as Alex helped me see, a good education, even if just for its own sake, is a worthy goal.

Danny Benjamin, 17

Part 5

Giving, Sharing, Making a Difference

Whatsoever things are right, just, pure, lovely or good . . . if there be virtue, if there be praise, report on these things.

—Philippians 4:8

The meaning of life is finding your gift; the purpose of life is giving it away.

—Joy J. Golliver

The spirit of charity exists in all of us. Sometimes the brightest sparks come from the smallest fires. There is power in every act of kindness, however small or grand.

—Deborah Spaide, founder, Kids Care Clubs

8 Why It Feels Good to Give

Do ordinary things with extraordinary love.

—Mother Teresa

FORTY-FOUR GLADIOLAS

One spring, while I was planting fifty gladiola bulbs, my six-year-old asked, "What are you planting, Mommy?"

"Gladiolas, honey," I answered. "My favorite flower."

"More than anything else?" she asked in wide-eyed innocence.

"More than anything else, honey," I replied.

"I wish I had given them to you," she lamented.

"Well, then," I remarked, playing into her need to show me her love, "Whichever ones you hand me, I will believe with all my heart they are from you!" There remained only six bulbs to plant.

The next week it was Mother's Day. To my surprise, my little daughter presented me with a gift, a white shoe box on which

she had drawn blooming flowers. Unable to contain her antici-
pation of my response to her gift, she put her small hands to her
glee-filled face and squealed in delight, "Now you can say ALL
of them are from me!" The box was filled with gladiola bulbs—
forty-four of them! My daughter had dug up the bulbs I had
planted the week prior—so that when I [re]planted them, they
would be from her.

Bettie B. Youngs

A Word from the Authors

"Mom, I can't believe you're telling that story about the forty-
four gladiolas in a book for teens. Besides, it makes me sound
like a little geek!"

"On the contrary, Jennifer, I think it's a darling story. And I
don't think it makes you look like a geek at all, but rather, points
out how natural it is to want to give. You were only a child, and
needed to show your love. Intuitively you knew that 'giving'
was a way to do that. Your gesture was innocent of all hidden
agenda, which makes it even that much more sweet."

"Giving *is* a sweet gesture, but besides that, it feels so good to
do things for others."

Luckily, the need to give never goes away. This past week, my
daughter, now twenty-four, handed me a bouquet of flowers,
watching intently for my reaction. When I swooned at the beauty of the flowers—and her gesture of giving them to me—her
eyes lit up and a beautiful ear-to-ear smile appeared. Buying the
flowers for me had elicited her joy, but seeing my happiness in
receiving them had made her joy complete.

In the stories in this chapter, you'll meet teens whose experiences, while sometimes vastly different from each other, all lead
to validating the phrase "It's more fun to give than receive."
Sixteen-year-old Steve Hand volunteered to spend "time" with a
group of young boys in a shelter, and discovered that it wasn't

his time that was valued as much as the bracelet he was wearing! And Mr. Paul, the school custodian, found out what students thought of his "time." After being voted Citizen-of-the-Year by the kids in his school, seventeen-year-old Kevin Lloyd thanked them, and then surprised everyone when he told them he wanted to share the award with someone special—Mr. Paul, the custodian. Shaking as he spoke, Mr. Paul humbly thanked the students and told them that in his entire life, it was the only award he'd ever received. With tears in his eyes, he walked off stage holding the plastic award as though it were a precious piece of crystal.

Robyn also received a gift—every couple of days as a matter of fact! Robyn thought they were left by "angels," but fourteen-year-old Paige Williams tells us who really left them! Thirteen-year-old Rhonda Klemmer made a difference to Cindy Lindburg when she told her she'd have more friends if she didn't "smell so bad." Fifteen-year-old Becky Coldwell did some explaining as well: "What goes around, comes around," her father had told her. When testing this principle, Becky detects something even *more* important.

All in all, teens discovered a simple truth about giving, sharing and doing things for others: While it made a difference in the lives of those they served, it also made a difference in their own. Sixteen-year-old Kevin Pauls said that helping others is a way to "earn a merit badge in life."

Teens say that kind words and actions are among the things we "give." They help make the world a "better place." Being kind and considerate can remind us that while we live in a world where someone may walk through a door and not hold it open for you, or someone may even take someone's life without any regard for it, many teens go out of their way to be courteous, kind and to assist each other. And to make the world a loving place in which to be.

And that's what being a "taste berry" is all about!

Citizen of the Year

My school held an annual end-of-the year awards assembly to recognize those students who, in one way or another, stood out because of their exceptional performance in sports, academics, extracurricular activities or who brought honor to the school in some way. As each award was handed out, the audience clapped, hooted, whistled and cheered wildly. Finally came the award for best citizenship, to be given to the person who had most contributed in a positive and significant way to our school.

The award went to Kevin Lloyd. He was not only on the football team, but was also student body vice-president and president of Youth for a Better Tomorrow. Kevin leaped up on stage, his customary enthusiasm and charisma present in his bright eyes and sincere smile. "Thanks," he said in the midst of our applause. "This is an honor, thank you. I appreciate this honor everyone—*but*," his voice rose to quiet the applause, "there's someone who deserves this more than I do."

The crowd grew silent at his unexpected words. "Someone who spends more hours at this school than any of us. Someone who gets here before we do, and he's here long after we're gone. Someone who can be found picking up a candy wrapper or a soda can carelessly discarded. Someone who has attended just about every special event, every football, baseball, basketball, softball and soccer game this school has held. You name it, he's there, cheering the team on, cleaning up before and after, taking pride in everything about this school. And he never lets that get in the way of offering a helping hand or giving a word of encouragement to any of us, either. I've seen him out in the parking lot helping a student change a tire. I've seen him walking students to the nurse's office when they didn't feel too well. I've seen him listen when someone just needed to talk. I've seen him offering encouragement to us kids to help us turn a 'bummer-of-a-day' attitude into a positive outlook. I've seem him joke with students, and I've seen him just listen and be there for a student with a broken heart, his own eyes looking as sad as the kid's. I've seen him search through garbage cans looking for an assignment that a student thought had been inadvertently thrown away. I could go on and on, but I don't need to. I'm sure you all know who I'm talking about—Mr. Paul—and I'd like to give this award to him."

Rising to their feet, the audience went wild, chanting, "Mr. Paul! Mr. Paul! Mr. Paul!" Mr. Paul looked a little embarrassed and overwhelmed, still he beamed as he was coaxed by students to get up on stage and take his award.

That day, Mr. Paul, our school's tireless and dedicated custodian, was named our *Citizen of the Year* to enthusiastic whoops of applause and approval.

Mr. Paul, with tears in his eyes, walked up and accepted the award, his words simple. "Thank you so much. I don't know what to say other than I've only done two important things in my whole entire life. The first was serving this fine school in a job I've loved. And the second was having you share this award with me, because it makes me realize that you know I love you all as much as I do."

With that, Mr. Paul, who in just three months would retire from the school district, stepped down. With his eyes still teary—and a smile that stretched from ear to ear—he held the plastic award as though it were a precious crystal. It was the only time he'd ever been publicly recognized for his dedication, his consistently thorough work, his endless acts of giving, and for a lifetime of service to others.

Remember, though, it took someone thoughtful and kind and secure in himself, like Kevin Lloyd, to make it happen.

Jennifer Leigh Youngs

The Girl No One Talked To

Last year there was a girl at our school who hardly anyone talked to. I think it was because she seldom showered, and she kind of smelled bad. Her name was Cindy Lindburg. I didn't know exactly where she lived, but it must have been somewhere in the neighborhood because we always got on the school bus at the same bus stop.

Cindy Lindburg didn't have many friends. She always came to the lunch room alone and she left alone. On the bus, no one offered her a seat, and she never asked if she could share a seat with others. I thought that maybe it was because she was sort of a shy person. She seemed like a nice girl—who had an odor problem.

One day, I was walking up to the bus stop and I saw Carl Littleton making fun of her. I couldn't hear what he was saying, but I saw the way he was laughing and rolling his eyes in his typical poking-fun-at-you way. I also saw how sad it made Cindy. Clutching her notebook to her chest like a shield, she stared at the ground and moved as far away from him as possible without leaving the bus stop entirely. As soon as I got close enough, I glared at Carl to make him stop laughing—even though I knew he probably wouldn't. He didn't, so I walked over and stood closer to Cindy so she wouldn't feel quite so bad. It was just one of those times when you just know someone needs someone to be a friend.

I didn't think she'd say anything, but she did. Her eyes peeked up from staring at the ground and as though she thought I'd be embarrassed if anyone heard her speak to me, she whispered "Hi."

"Hi," I said. Then as loudly as I could, I said, "Don't pay any attention to Carl. His parents have been unsuccessful in teaching him some manners."

Some of the kids standing there laughed. The comment didn't even rouse a smile out of Cindy. By now everyone there was talking with a friend. Quietly, and with a serious look on her face, Cindy said, "I don't know why everyone hates me."

I was surprised at her words. "No one hates you," I told her.

"Then why don't I have any friends?" she asked.

Her question took me by surprise. I thought for a moment. "Well," I began, wondering if I could tell her that maybe it was because she smelled so awful, "I think you're really nice and I think that the kids at school think you're smart and all, and you dress okay, and . . ."

"So then, what is it?" she blurted.

"Well," I hedged and then figured it's now or never. "Maybe it's because you. . . ." I paused because I almost said "stink" but said instead, "don't smell so good."

She looked up, studying my face as if checking to see if I was making fun of her or being mean. I guess she decided I wasn't. She nodded, like she believed what I said was true. Since she seemed to take this well, I added, "I think you'd probably make more friends if you took more baths." She looked away and, worried that I might have gone too far, I shrugged and added, "It's just a thought." (My mom says that sometimes when she gives me advice.)

Turning back to face me, Cindy took a deep breath and said, "Thank you."

I was so relieved, and the next moment the bus arrived, and all the kids started piling on.

"If I save a seat for you on the bus tomorrow," she asked, "will you sit with me?"

"Sure," I said.

I'm happy to report that Cindy did take more baths from that day on. And it wasn't too long before she started to make friends at school. I was one of them.

I made a difference for the better in Cindy's life. And got a new friend to boot!

Rhonda Klemmer, 14

"No Big Deal!"

Last year our class went to the roller rink as a reward for having perfect attendance for a full semester. It was the first time I had ever been to a roller rink. I loved it, but I had a hard time standing up on the skates. I kept falling down, and some of the other kids laughed at me.

A lady who works at the snack bar called me over and gave me a free soda. All she said was, "Looks like you need this." As she talked, she counted out coins from the apron she was wearing. It probably was her tip money. She rang up the soda, paying for it with her money.

I guess she'd seen me falling—and the kids laughing. I thanked her.

"No big deal," she said. "You looked like you could use cheering up!"

It worked. As the other kids watched me get my free soda, I didn't feel like such a clumsy jerk. And I think they must have thought I was someone special to have someone just hand me a soda—one I didn't have to pay for.

That soda made a big difference to me. For the rest of the time I was there, no one said a word when I fell down—some kids even boosted me up as they skated by and saw that I was about to fall. Some even reached out to pull me along with them!

Just one person, even someone I didn't know, taking the trouble to notice that I felt embarrassed and then doing something to cheer me up, made me feel better. It made a real difference to me.

She may have said "no big deal," but a soda on that day was a big deal to me!

Mark Howard, 12

Not Always to the Sender

My father uses the expression, "What goes around comes around." He says that when we're good to others or do good things for them, they're usually good to us back. But my mother says a payback for a good deed doesn't always come back to the sender, but sometimes, to someone else. I think they both may be right.

Three weeks ago, as I was going to class, I saw Gia Hayes making a mad dash to class when suddenly her books and papers slipped from her arms and went flying every which way down the hallway. Gia became so frustrated that all she could do was stand there and cry. So I stopped to help Gia gather her things.

Helping Gia made me late to Mrs. Wentworth's class. I was scared, too, because Mrs. Wentworth is a very strict teacher. You can't be even one minute late to her class without getting a detention, which means you have to stay after school ten minutes for every minute you're late to class. But on that day, for some reason, Mrs. Wentworth didn't say a thing. She wasn't upset and she didn't keep me after school. You can imagine how relieved I was! I'd like to think that was my payback for helping Gia; like my dad says, "what goes around comes around"—and mine came from Mrs. Wentworth.

That very same afternoon, I saw something that made me think about what my mother says, about how payback for a good deed doesn't always come back to the sender, but can come back to someone else.

I was sitting on the bus after school when I saw Lindsey Deutch, running as fast as she could so she'd reach the bus before it took off. She lost her footing and slipped and fell down, practically landing on her face. I mean, her whole body was flat against the ground. It must have hurt, too. As she scrambled to her feet, straightening her backpack over her shoulder, I could see a big rip all the way down the back of her skirt. I could also see her horror as she discovered it herself. Right then, along came Gia Hayes. Gia took one look at Lindsey's problem, whipped off her sweater and gave it to Lindsey to wrap around her hips.

You never know just how, where or when a good deed will come back to you. But I do know we could all make the world a better place to live in just by all of us doing our share of good things. That doesn't seem all that difficult to do.

Becky Coldwell, 15

9

One by One by One . . . Makes a Difference Collectively

Do all the good you can, by all the means you can,
in all the ways you can, in all the places you can,
at all the times you can, to all the people you can,
as long as you ever can.

—John Wesley

THE STARFISH

A man was jogging on the beach one day when he came across a boy picking up starfish and frantically slinging them into the ocean. "I'm afraid your efforts are in vain, young man!" the jogger said as he approached the boy. "Hundreds of starfish have been washed ashore here, and they're withering fast in the hot sun. Your well-intentioned efforts simply aren't going to make a difference. You might as well run along and play."

The boy surveyed the many starfish stranded on the beach, then looked at the beautiful starfish he was holding. Flinging it into the ocean, he replied optimistically, "Well, I made a difference to that one!"

A Word from the Authors

"I love this little story, Mom, because it illuminates an ideal we must each take to heart: There is great significance and importance in all our day-to-day actions in both words and deeds."

"That's right, Jennifer. Just as the boy's singular actions made a difference to each individual starfish he touched, we each make a difference one person at a time, one by one by one."

A reporter once asked Mother Teresa, one of the greatest "taste berries" of our times, what she considered to be the single most important thing we can do to make the world a better place. Her answer was simply, "Begin with one single act of kindness—in your family, in your community and everywhere you go. Just begin . . . one, one, one."

As you'll see by the stories in this chapter, teens are making a difference all over the world, one by one by one. Seventeen-year-old Cara Robinson gave up her place in line at the post office and unknowingly saved a mother and her two young children from having the heat turned off in their apartment. Fifteen-year-old Carrie Hague provided "Fred in the Green Shirt" the much-needed exercise he needed to "stay alive"; twelve-year-old Brian Lumke explains the global importance of his rescuing a lizard from the paws of his cat. A "hungry" fourteen-year-old Mike Siciliano tells how thirty hours of hunger helped an elderly woman receive the home cleaning and repairs she needed, and Sadie Murray, fifteen, tells you what she did in exchange for a share in a "stash" of Bazooka bubble gum.

"You know, Mom, I especially enjoyed working on this section of the book because there is something about helping others that just brings out the best in each of us. I'm so happy to include this chapter because I once heard that 95 percent of the news coverage focused on youth is about those involved in drugs, violence and negative gangs, yet only 5 percent of teens ever commit those kind of acts. It seems like teens easily attract attention if they do something wrong, but, in fact, 95 percent of the teens are doing good things. I'm reminded of a story I heard Rabbi Wayne Dosick tell about when his home recently burned to the ground in a wildfire. He said it wasn't just family, friends and the Red Cross who came to his family's aid, but also a group of kids in his neighborhood. They took up a collection of their own money and raised three hundred dollars, then went to the local hardware store to buy tools their neighbors would need to dig through the ashes. When the manager of the store heard what they were doing, he matched their three hundred dollars! As news of what they were doing spread through the store, other customers began donating money, and another five hundred dollars was raised. The next day, all of the kids piled into one of the store's trucks and drove through the neighborhood handing out all the tools to their neighbors—over eleven hundred dollars in shovels, rakes, work gloves, wastebaskets and garbage bags. Teens are thoughtful, helpful and loving."

"Yes, they are, Jennifer, and I think that story makes the point that so many young people are doing such good things."

One act, one word, one person and one day at a time, the stories in this chapter prove that teens are up to the challenge of making a positive difference in the world. Teens involved with Habitat for Humanity travel to places they've never been, with others they've never met, to do something they've never done—namely, build houses from start to finish in two weeks. Like so many other teens, they learn that when joining together for a common purpose, people can accomplish great things.

Everywhere you turn, "taste-berry" teens are helping others. And the effects are far-reaching. There is no absence of "taste berries" in today's teens! Want to get involved? Teens had some great suggestions about the many ways to get involved in doing, giving and making a difference! Authors Joy J. Golliver and Ruth Hayes-Arista have written a book on 301 ways teens can turn caring into action. [See the end of chapter 9.] Check it out!

"Fred in the Green Shirt"

I had only three hours of community service work left for a school project. I was happy to be completing the hours, but bummed that the time it was scheduled for was a bright, sunny Saturday afternoon. I would have preferred to be doing other things.

As my mother dropped me off at the home for elderly Alzheimer's patients where I was to complete my hours, I secretly wished I could leave. "There are so many other places I would rather be," I thought.

Luckily, I willed myself to stay. It turned out to be a very special day.

I was handed a beach ball and told that my first job was to find "Fred in the green shirt" and play "catch the ball" with him. Having been given these instructions, the nurse pointed in the direction of the patio.

I walked onto the patio to find "Fred in the green shirt." He was sitting in a chair, staring into the garden. I asked him if he wanted to play ball. He just looked at me blankly. So I gently tossed the ball at him. A big smile came across his face and as he reached to grab the ball, he almost fell out of his chair. He needed help to stand up, so I helped him up. He stood there grinning at me and then suddenly threw the ball back to me. This went on for about ten minutes, each minute seeming to take forever. It was really a chore for him to concentrate so hard and then to think about each action in tossing the ball back to me.

It was such a monotonous game, and I wondered if he was getting bored with it. My doubts didn't last long. With a serious look on his face he broke the silence with the words, "Good exercise!" And then, with tears in his eyes, he added, "Helps stay alive." The other seniors who had gathered to watch murmured their agreement. Then, all heads turning in my direction, they smiled at me.

In that moment, I knew my afternoon was being well spent. I completed my service hours with a better, happier attitude. I was being helpful after all. Fred needed exercise and was happy that I was patiently providing it.

When it was time for Fred to take a break, he thanked me wholeheartedly—not with words, but with the gratitude and appreciation in his eyes. And it was really important to him that he and I shake hands. "Again, soon," he said, shaking his head with enthusiasm. "Again, soon."

I know that what I did was a simple thing, but I also know that it meant something to someone else. I could see it in his eyes, and in his smile. And it was evident in the seniors who watched with interest as I played ball with him. I believe that what I did was much more than playing ball; by my presence, I had shown an interest in another. I could see that they were thankful and grateful. For Fred getting the exercise—and for me for giving it.

"Fred in the green shirt" was a lesson I won't soon forget. It taught me that all of us—no matter how old or how young, no matter what health condition we are in—need others to show an interest, and to be patient and tolerant. I learned that a simple act of caring can make a difference. I want to believe that I made a difference to Fred that day. And I maybe even made a difference to his children or grandchildren, who would feel good that their father or grandfather had some attention and exercise that day.

Now I stop in at the center every now and then, even without needing hours for a project as motivation for volunteering. And always I check up on "Fred in the green shirt"—who claps his hands in joy the moment he sees me, then searches my hands to see if they're holding a ball.

Which they usually are!

Carrie Hague, 15

Keeping the Heat On

Three weeks ago, I was in the post office buying stamps for a couple of letters I wanted to send. A woman with two very young children was standing in line behind me. Her little kids were cranky and wanted no part of standing in a line. The mother looked as tired and harried as her kids. So, I told the woman she could go before me. She thanked me and got in line in front of me.

There's a cutoff point for serving people at the window of the post office, and it was just a few minutes to closing time. Unfortunately, the line wasn't moving very fast and a postal clerk closed the line off right behind her and before me. His decision meant that I wasn't going to get my letters mailed out that day—and all because I let her get in line in front of me!

At first, I was upset that I had given up my place in line, especially because it meant I'd have to come back another day. But when the woman turned to me and said, "I feel bad that you've been inconvenienced because you gave up your place in line. But I want to thank you for being so courteous. If the payment for my heating bill wasn't postmarked by today, the gas and electric company was going to turn the heat off in my apartment."

By letting her go first, I had made a difference to her and her two small children.

Probably we don't always know when the little things we do make a difference to others, but after learning what it meant to that woman, and how it saved her from having her heat turned off, I've decided to be more thoughtful to others, and to just assume that in some way, it probably mattered to them.

I believe that if we all practice being courteous, if goodwill is our motto, then we can make a really big difference in the world.

When I left the post office, I was not at all upset for the inconvenience of driving there, parking and waiting in line. Instead, I left feeling really good. My having to go back the next day was definitely worth it. Since that day, I've definitely continued to look for ways to help others whenever possible, in whatever small ways I can.

Cara Robinson, 17

There Are Lots of Ways to Help Others

My little sister, Carrie, is only nine. Once a month she takes her dog, Pal, to a children's home where the little kids take turns holding and petting her dog. One time I had to drive her there because our mother couldn't. A little boy put Pal on his lap and petted him—while he was taking chemotherapy. I heard chemotherapy burns really bad. Petting Carrie's dog helped distract the little boy from the pain of the chemotherapy. To that little boy that day, Pal was a welcome sight.

A lot of my friends "think globally," they just don't know what do to "act locally." What my little sister does with her dog proves there are lots of ways to help others. All you have to do is look around you and see how other people are serving others. Like my family, for example.

My mother gives the clothes our family doesn't need to our local church. Every few months or so, we do the clean-your-closet routine. I always find something that I don't need, don't like or I've outgrown, things someone else should be using. Just this last time, I dug out my shoes. I had two pairs of cleats. One pair I may use again this next season (if I don't outgrow them) and the other pair is already too small. It's not like I need this second pair. I don't have a brother, and my little sister isn't going to ever wear cleats. I'll just bet there's some kid out there who would love to own a pair but can't afford them. So, I "donated" the second pair of cleats.

Another thing our family does is sponsor an animal (a giraffe named Shorty) at the zoo. Each month we write out a check for forty-five dollars and send it in. The money goes toward Shorty's food bill. Even my older sister, Sheree, who's twenty-two and who is really busy, still finds time to volunteer. She works for the airlines and is active in a group called the Airline Ambassadors; they donate their time and flight miles to help families of sick or injured children get the medical attention they need.

So I've learned to keep my eyes open when it comes to looking for what I can do to help others. Right now I'm involved with a group in my school, headed by one of the counselors. We're organizing a neighborhood drive where each family donates one nonperishable item or canned good on the last day of every month. There are less than twenty homes in my neighborhood, so I can cover these in probably three or four hours on a Saturday or Sunday afternoon. The food is picked up by a group called Meals on Wheels, an organization that donates food to seniors in need of food. I've discovered I like going around to collect the food—it gives me a chance to talk to everyone in the neighborhood. I'm good at it and it's good for the cause. I like it so much that I'm making a commitment to stay involved in the group for at least a year.

Helping is an attitude, more than anything else. If a person is open to helping others, usually you'll find the opportunity right at the tip of your nose.

Randy Bobrow, 16

Help Abused or Abandoned Animals

When it comes to making a difference in the world, I'm most interested in doing it by helping animals. Every community has a shelter for abandoned or abused animals. Just ask around or look in the yellow pages, and you'll find one. You can check out *www.planetpets.simplenet.com* for a list of *101 Things You Can Do to Save Animals*. There are many groups that work to help and protect all different kinds of animals. I know in my community alone, we have six animal shelters and a bird sanctuary. You can donate time to help comfort and care for the animals, or you can donate supplies or pet food.

Every month I send five dollars to one of the animal shelters in my town; and then I help walk Mrs. Hemmeter's dog, Buster. Mrs. Hemmeter is getting really old and she can't walk Buster for herself anymore—but other than that she can take care of Buster just fine. So my stopping by and taking Buster for a walk keeps them together and makes them both happy.

If you're really into animals, like I am, there are also temporary pets available. For example, in my community there is a group called Canine Companions for Independence. This group is always looking for help training puppies and, sometimes, grown dogs. Golden retrievers, Labrador retrievers and sheltie puppies are placed with volunteer puppy raisers at eight weeks of age and are returned to the training center for advanced training at six to eight months. I think it would be so much fun to volunteer as a puppy raiser. My parents aren't going for it right now, but I still think it would be such an awesome thing to be able to do.

When it comes to volunteering, let's not forget the other creatures on our planet who depend on our help, too!

Danny Joseph, 15

You! Yes, You!

If you want to know more ways you can take action to help others, as its title promises, *I Can Ignite the Community Spirit: 301 Ways to Turn Caring into Action*, by Joy J. Golliver and Ruth Hayes-Arista, is a marvelous resource—and will give you 301 ways. You can order it by calling 800-254-ICAN, or writing I CAN Ignite the Community Spirit, 500 West Roy Street, #W107, Seattle, Washington 98119.

Here's just one example of how practical and useful this book is. Under the ways to help the homeless, we found:

ACTION! When walking down the street, rather than giving money, respond with kindness. Try a kind word to bolster their self-confidence and self-worth. Society benefits from their increased self-esteem.

ACTION! Keep a shopping bag in your closet. Every time you go to the grocery, buy something for your shopping bag that can be used by a homeless person. If you get a gift you know you will never use, put it in your shopping bag. Things that you outgrow or do not wear and are not needed by your family, put in the bag. When the bag is full, drop it off at a shelter for the homeless.

ACTION! On your own birthday, buy birthday cards and add a note that reads "To celebrate my birthday, I wanted to give you a gift so that you can have a special day when your birthday arrives." Put some money in the card and distribute to homeless men and women and children.

ACTION! Be a role model to your friends and neighbors. Volunteer at a soup kitchen or food bank. Make it an event for family and friends. Meeting the homeless face to face proves that they're people just like us, just experiencing some bad luck.

ACTION! Support creative projects in your community.

Organize new projects. Street Wise is a newspaper sold in some communities by the homeless. A similar publication is Real Changes. The homeless can get the first ten newspapers free and sell them for one dollar. When they invest that ten dollars in more newspapers they receive forty newspapers for twenty-five cents each and sell them for a profit of seventy-five cents and keep the money. This a well-organized project. Workers sign an employment contract and are licensed by the city. This gives them a step up and a sense of self-worth. If such a program is not in your community, why not help to start one? If it is in your community, buy newspapers and support the homeless that are working.

ACTION! Show your compassion and caring. Start in your own home. Care about your brothers and sisters. Show them love and respect and consideration. Next, become a Big Sister or Big Brother to a needy child in your community. You just may be the one person in their lives who provides the motivation, encouragement—and love—that will help someone face life's challenges without becoming homeless.

About the Authors

Bettie B. Youngs, Ph.D., Ed.D., is a professional speaker and the internationally renowned author of sixteen books translated into twenty-nine languages. She is a former Teacher of the Year, university professor and executive director of the Phoenix Foundation. Currently, she is president of Professional Development, Inc. She is a long-acknowledged expert on teens and has frequently appeared on *NBC Nightly News*, CNN, *Oprah* and *Geraldo*. *USA Today*, the *Washington Post, Redbook, McCall's, Working Woman, Family Circle, Parents Magazine, Better Homes & Gardens, Woman's Day* and the National Association for Secondary School Principals (NASSP) have all recognized her work. Her acclaimed books include *Safeguarding Your Teenager from the Dragons of Life; How to Develop Self-Esteem in Your Child; Stress and Your Child: Helping Kids Cope with the Strains and Pressures of Life; You and Self-Esteem: A Book for Young People; Taste-Berry Tales; Gifts of the Heart;* and the award-winning *Values from the Heartland*. Dr. Youngs is the author of a number of video-cassette programs for Sybervision and Nightingale/Conant and the coauthor of the nationally acclaimed *Parents on Board*, a video-based training program to help schools and parents work together to increase student achievement.

Jennifer Leigh Youngs, twenty-four, is a speaker and work-shop presenter for teens and parents nationwide. She is the author of *A Stress-Management Guide for Young People* and the co-author of *Goal-Setting Skills for Young Adults* and *Problem-Solving Skills for Children*. Jennifer is a former Miss Teen California finalist and a Rotary International Goodwill Ambassador and

Exchange Scholar. She serves on a number of advisory boards for teens including the National Advisory Board for Caboodles International. Her interests focus on the well-being of teens. "I'd like to be happy, to live my life around those things that seem meaningful to me, and I'd especially like those who meet me—even if for a brief moment—to feel they met a friend," she says.

To contact Bettie Youngs or Jennifer Leigh Youngs, write to:

Bettie B. Youngs & Associates
Box 2588
Del Mar, CA 92014